ZION'S HOPE

PIONEER MIDWIVES

&

WOMEN DOCTORS OF UTAH

HONEY M. NEWTON, CNM

CFI

AN IMPRINT OF CEDAR FORT, INC.

SPRINGVILLE, UTAH

*This book is dedicated to my eternal
companion, to my sweet children, and to
all those who give of themselves to bring
new life into the world.*

ISBN 13: 978-1-4621-1129-9

Published by CFI, an imprint of Cedar Fort, Inc., 2373 W. 700 S., Springville, UT 84663
Distributed by Cedar Fort, Inc., www.cedarfort.com

Library of Congress Cataloging-in-Publication Data on File

Cover design by Angela D. Olsen
Cover design © 2013 by Lyle Mortimer
Edited and typeset by Whitney A. Lindsley

Printed in the United States of America

10 9 8 7 6 5 4 3 2 1

CONTENTS

MEDICAL PRACTICE AND MIDWIFERY IN EARLY UTAH

CHILDBEARING ON THE WESTERN FRONTIER was often filled with difficulty and danger. Early pioneer settlers had to rely on the help and skills of those nearest them, whether they had formal training or not. The women who gave birth in wagon trains usually had only a few hours to recover before resuming the trek. Women in fledgling settlements bore their children in harsh conditions, often in shacks with dirt floors and few resources. To answer their need, midwives of all descriptions began assisting their neighbors during the confinement period. They also became the local doctors, attending to old and young, setting bones, treating illness, and performing minor surgeries. Some charged two or three dollars for a delivery with ten days care of the household, and others gave their services freely. We see exceptionally intelligent women who defied social norms to return east and attend medical school, and we see humble lay midwives who gained expertise through the refining fire of experience.

During the late nineteenth century, a larger proportion of female physicians were in Utah than anywhere else in the world, with the possible exception of Russia. The natural aversion of Victorian-era women to having a male attend them during birth strengthened the domination of women in medicine throughout the Territory of Utah and nearby locales. Indeed, Utah's first hospital and Department of Health were organized and run

by female midwives and physicians and sponsored by the Latter-day Saint Relief Society. Some midwives even took to the profession when their stake president called them. In the late 1860s, Brigham Young assigned two of his wives the task of promoting health education and training midwives. In 1873, he determined that each ward's Relief Society should ask three women to study nursing and midwifery, and a school of nursing was opened to facilitate this. This same year, the first women went to study at eastern medical schools. The most well-known women were Romania Pratt, Ellis Reynolds Shipp, and Ellen B. Ferguson, among others. Dr. Pratt wrote many articles on health and educated a new generation of midwives. Dr. Shipp is known for her school of obstetrics and nursing, and her care of the poor. She also created the first medical journal in Utah. One of the first female physicians in Utah was Dr. Ellen B. Ferguson (April 10, 1844– March 17, 1920), a native of England. Besides her busy medical practice, she was also the first female deputy sheriff in the United States[1] and an ardent feminist. She desperately wanted to bring true medicine to the West. The dream of Dr. Ferguson became a reality when the Deseret Hospital opened in 1882.

"By 1900, there were at least 34 female and 236 male doctors practicing medicine in Utah."[2] The prominent role of midwives began to slowly fade, though they remained secure in the hearts of those that they helped. Midwives and women physicians continue to care for women and children in Utah today, working in hospitals, birthing centers, and homes. The tradition of service by our foremothers whispers to all of us and urges us on . . . to give of our time, knowledge, and skills, to rise at the eleventh hour to answer a cry for help, to keep the faith and work for a brighter Zion.

Note: In every case the author has endeavored to include autobiographical sources. When this is not possible, these stories are taken from accounts of descendants, recorded interviews, collections in the *Utah Historical Quarterly*, archived histories in the possession of the Daughters of the Utah Pioneers, and journals. The author was not able to pay tribute to every pioneer midwife and woman doctor. Please see Appendix A for further information.

NOTES

1. Blanche E. Rose, "Early Utah Medical Practice: Women Doctors, Ellen B. Ferguson," *Utah Historical Quarterly* 10 (1942): 29.

2. *Encyclopedia of Mormonism*, s.v. "Maternity and Child Health Care," accessed January 5, 2010, http://www.lightplanet.com/mormons/daily/health/Maternity_Child_EOM.htm.

PROLOGUE

"Who can find a virtuous woman?
For her price is far above rubies." (Proverbs 31:10)

EARLY PIONEER MIDWIVES AND WOMEN DOC-tors had a deep and lasting impact on the expansion of the West. They manifested a diversity of knowledge, ethnicity, and economic position. Some began their professions by answering the plea of a neighbor in distress, while others broke through gender stereotypes to graduate with honors from prestigious medical programs. The common thread among them was their resilient faith and their desire to serve others. These sisters provided compassionate care to anyone who called on them—from the cradle to the grave—rarely receiving recompense for their efforts. They crossed thousands of miles on foot with their own families in tow. The services they provided eased the suffering of the sick, brought new life into the world, and softened the burden of its passing.

The life histories of these women are rarely told, becoming a hazy memory or a scrap of journal in a descendant's closet. Few of these women, were they alive today, would desire a public accolade. They humbly went about their work in bitter weather, through seasons of pestilence, and under threat of war, day and night, year after year. They rejoiced at the lusty cry of a newborn and wept when death closed the eyes of a patient too soon. Without exception, they raised families and worked the land, coaxing a harvest from the harsh soil of this new place called Zion. They were not born of privilege or power. They remain exceptional for how they chose to spend the time granted them on earth. As this tribute will reveal, pioneer midwives

and women doctors of Utah and the surrounding area were supreme examples of Christlike service. This collection of stories is meant to inspire and uplift, lest we forget their sacrifice.

PATTY BARTLETT SESSIONS

(February 4, 1795–December 14, 1892)

*". . . that I may do good to myself and all others while I live,
this is my prayer."*[1]

IDWIFE, HEALER, DEVOTED MOTHER, scholar, pioneer, faithful covert, expert gardener, business-woman, and leader—many words describe the talents of Patty Bartlett Sessions. Born on February 4, 1795, during a frigid Maine winter, Patty was the oldest of Enoch and Martha Ann Hall Bartlett's nine children. Her parents recognized her sharp wit and strong work ethic and provided her with an education, which would serve her throughout her life. Showing her stalwart determination, she married David Sessions at age seventeen, against her parents' counsel. The young couple had little besides enthusiasm, but they quickly established themselves, and in a few years, they became the support for David's parents. At this time, Patty began to learn the skills of a midwife.[2] She accomplished her first delivery quite by accident, when her mother-in-law was called to two different homes at once and

Patty was left alone to perform skills she had only observed before. The local physician arrived some time later and was impressed enough with her efforts to encourage Patty to pursue the practice of midwifery. As time passed, the Sessions family began to be financially prosperous owing to their hard work. Patty faithfully recorded her life in a daily journal. She chronicled more than four decades of entries, recording births, deaths, financial transactions, her travels through and settlement of the wilderness, and most important, her spiritual experiences and the thoughts of her heart.[3]

Patty and David were blessed with eight children, though only three survived to adulthood. Several epidemics ravaged the New England countryside during this time, and one by one they laid their sweet babes in the rocky soil. Patty's heart and mind readily accepted the gospel in 1834, when missionaries for the Church first began preaching in the area. Her husband accepted the truth as well, and they sold their farm, mill, and luxuries to gather with the Saints. The family settled in Far West, Missouri, where they experienced cruel persecutions that forced them to flee for their lives to Nauvoo, Illinois, abandoning all they owned. The journey was so harsh that tiny Amanda, born in Far West during happier days, would not survive the trip. Starting again from nothing, Patty and David built a home in Nauvoo. Despite her losses, Patty writes in her journal, "*I think I can take the spoiling of my things with joy.*"[4]

After the martyrdom of the Prophet Joseph Smith, Patty heeded the call to head west. Recognizing Patty's expert healing skills, Brigham Young asked Patty to accompany the pilot group. He set her apart as a midwife and called her to care for all who were sick and afflicted. Her entries speak of her round-the-clock service: "*I was caled [sic] to PP Pratts 1 oclock this morning Delivered Mary Pratt of a son [Helaman],*" and "*[Brother] Greys carried me across the water on his back, put his wife to bed with a daughter.*"[5] Patty knew the joys and hardships of polygamy, her entries revealing the close kinships of sisterhood and the gospel, and the struggles of human nature. She was not afraid to give all she had, despite the pain those risks often entailed. On one evening she writes, "*the sun came out, dried my bed, but my tears will not dry up.*"[6] Prompted by the Spirit to remember the past, she later writes, "*I feel bad yet my trust is in God he is my all . . .*"[7] After helping the Saints in Winter Quarters during the winter of 1846–47, she, at the age of fifty-two, arrived in Salt Lake "*[having driven her] waggon all the way but part of the two last [mountain]*" and had walked 1,030 miles.[8] On the day of her departure for the Salt Lake Valley, she wrote, "*we start for the mountains today and leave Winter Quarters, ten years today since we left our home and*

friends in Maine, we now leave many good friends and I hope they soon follow us, we started for a resting place, we knew not where."[9]

Patty and her family immediately began to settle and farm an area now known as North Salt Lake, growing staple crops and a carefully nurtured orchard. Soon after their establishment, David became ill and died. Patty's resilience shows in her journal entry: *"Mr. Sessions my husband died. After his death I built me a house where I now live."* After the death of her husband, Patty was sealed to John Parry, the first director of the Mormon Tabernacle Choir, in 1852.[10]

She actively served in the Church as president of the Indian Relief Society, among many other callings. Concerned with the education of many of the children she brought into the world, she funded the Patty Sessions Academy in Bountiful. Patty made rugs for the Salt Lake Tabernacle, contributed generously to the care of the poor, and was a member of the Council of Health, established by Willard Richards, which was to become the first Department of Health in the United States. She was known for her frugality, but would consistently give to the utmost farthing when asked. She recorded, *"Put my name in to give all I have to the church."*[11]

She continued to deliver babies until the age of eighty-five, recording an astounding 3,997 births. She enjoyed good health until her passing at age ninety-seven in 1892. In her later entries, she writes, *"When we came to this valley I had one five cent piece which I picked up on the red [Butte] and since Mr Sessions died, I have took care of myself and have laid up considerable. I have always paid my tithing, fasts . . . and all other demands. . . . And some donations when not called upon I gave liberally. I have done these with a willing heart and hand and the Lord has blessed me in basket and in my store."*[12]

Two sons—Peregrine (1814–1893), who founded Bountiful, Utah, and David Jr. (1823–1896)—survived her, her daughter, Sylvia, having passed away in 1882. She lived to see the fourth generation, her descendants numbering 33 grandchildren, 137 great-grandchildren and 22 great-great-grandchildren. This amazing pioneer woman left us a legacy of sacrifice and devotion, hard work, and true compassion toward all.[13]

"And I have to say to my Grand children and Great Grand children. Be faithful in paying your tithing. . . . And responding to every call made by the Authorities. . . . Be faithful in your Prayers in your families. . . . Do right let the result follow. And the Lord will bless you with wisdom, knowledge, and intel-[l]igence. Riches, Honor, and every good thing that your hearts can desire in righteousness. Teach your lit[t]le ones to pray as soon as they can lipse a prayer. And they will call down blessings upon your heads."[14]

NOTES

1.   Donna Toland Smart, ed., *Mormon Midwife: The Diaries of Patty Bartlett Sessions*. Salt Lake City: Utah University Press, 1997), 199.

2.   Ibid.

3.   Claire Noall, "Mormon Midwives," *Utah Historical Quarterly* 10 (1942), 84.

4.   *Mormon Midwife*, 199.

5.   Ibid., 254.

6.   Ibid., 52, 331.

7.   Ibid., 32.

8.   Ibid., 131.

9.   Ibid., 99, 343.

10.   Ibid., 343.

11.   Ibid.

12.   Ibid., 203.

13.   Ibid., 342.

14.   Ibid., 397.

15.   Ibid., 342.

BRIDGET "BIDDY" MASON

August 15, 1818–January 15, 1891

"The open hand is blessed, for it gives in abundance,
even as it receives."[1]

BRIDGET "BIDDY" MASON WAS BORN INTO SLAVery on a plantation in Hancock County, Georgia, on August 15, 1818. Separated from her parents as a child, she spent her early years working on John Smithson's plantation in South Carolina, where she learned midwifery and healing skills from the other African servants.[2] She and her two-year-old daughter, Ellen, were acquired by Robert Marion Smith and Rebecca Crosby in 1836. Settling in Mississippi, Biddy worked hard caring for Rebecca, who was frequently ill. She also acted as the local midwife in addition to her labors in the cotton fields and with the livestock. During this time, she bore two more daughters, Ann in 1844 and Harriet in 1848, reputedly fathered by her owner.[3]

Missionaries taught the Smith family, and in 1844, Robert and his family were baptized members of The Church of Jesus Christ of Latter-day Saints. The practice of baptizing and ordaining blacks during Joseph Smith's lifetime was discontinued after his death, and Biddy and the other household slaves were unable to experience these ordinances. At the time of Robert's conversion, members were told to free any slaves that they owned, but he chose to ignore this counsel.

In the spring of 1848, the Smith household left Mississippi to join a group of Saints fleeing Nauvoo for their new home in the Rocky Mountains.

With her infant bundled to her, Biddy began the two-thousand-mile journey along the Overland Trail with her ten-year-old daughter walking beside and her four-year-old holding her skirts. All slaves in the company had to walk behind the livestock on the hot dusty trail and were only offered water after the animals were satiated. Each night, she and the other thirty-four slaves in the party were responsible for setting up camp, preparing the food, and washing and tending to all the needs of the camp. Biddy delivered the children born to both slaves and white women on this seven-month journey.[4]

After spending a year in Salt Lake, Robert Smith was asked to join a group building a Mormon community in San Bernadino, California. President Brigham Young strongly exhorted Robert to free his slaves prior to his departure, counsel that Robert again ignored.[5] But unbeknownst to Smith, California had become a free state under the Constitution of 1849. In 1851, the Smith household arrived and established themselves in the growing community. It is here that we begin to catch glimpses of Biddy's desires and intentions. She sought to learn how to obtain freedom for herself and others, all the while securing her reputation as a midwife and healer through hard work. Several free blacks who had traveled to California from Utah told Biddy how to obtain her freedom and began to file petitions on her behalf, since she was unable to read or write. Among them were Charles and Elizabeth Rowan, Manuel Pepper, and Charles Owens, who wished to marry Biddy's daughter Ellen.[6] Robert Smith had grown tired of the anti-slavery sentiment in his area and was disaffected from the Church over a financial and land dispute with the local clergy. He decided to move to the state of Texas, where slavery was still widely practiced.[7] In 1855, he packed up his household and fled the valley but was delayed in the mountains, where the group had to stop to wait for another of Smith's slaves, Hannah, to deliver her eighth child. A local posse caught up with them and issued Robert a writ of *habeas corpus*, taking the slaves into custody for their protection. Robert maintained that the slaves were not property, but instead simply members of his family. A two-day trial began, with Smith declaring that all the slaves desired to go to Texas and remain forever in servitude. After meeting with Biddy privately to hear her story, Los Angeles County District Judge Benjamin Hayes set Biddy and all of the other slaves free on January 21, 1856.[8]

Free and homeless, Biddy was invited to live with the family of Robert Owens. As a free woman, she was finally allowed to take a surname. She chose the name "Mason" in honor of her longtime friend and Mormon apostle Amasa Lyman, with whom she had spent a great deal of time.[9] Mason

was the middle name of Amasa, who was currently serving as mayor of San Bernadino. Biddy was offered employment by Dr. John Strother Griffin,[10] who was impressed with her character and abilities, for the unheard of wage of $2.50 a day.[11] Biddy carefully saved the money she earned as a midwife and became the first African American woman to purchase land in the city.[12] On November 28, 1866, Biddy purchased two lots in what is now the commercial district of Los Angeles. She built several small wooden houses and rented out the spaces for extra income. Biddy did not enjoy a house of her own until she was sixty-six.[13] As a result of her frugality and business sense, Biddy became the wealthiest African American woman in Los Angeles.[14] She rose to upper social circles, even dining on occasion with the wealthy Pio Pico, the last governor of Mexican California.

Biddy used her wealth and influence to bless the lives of others, donating much of her fortune to worthy causes. She was known for giving her services away to those who couldn't pay and became affectionately known as "Grandma" or "Aunt."[15] Biddy devoted her remaining years to caring for the needy. In addition to delivering babies day and night, healing the sick, and feeding the unfortunate who would line up in front of her house, she is reputed to have founded a travelers' aid center and an orphanage. Illiterate herself, she used money from her real estate investments to build an elementary school for African American children. She taught herself Spanish in order to better care for some of her patients in the multiracial colony. Toward the end of her life, she was asked to finance the founding the First African Methodist Episcopal Church, the cities first and now oldest African American church.[16] Biddy saved nearly $300,000 during her life, much of which she donated to local schools, churches, and charities. Despite her life of service, Biddy was buried in an unmarked grave in the Evergreen Cemetery after her death on January 15, 1891. One hundred years later, the first African American Mayor of Los Angeles, Tom Bradley, placed a headstone over her grave and declared November 16 as "Biddy Mason Day."[17] There is now a community building on the site of her home and a large memorial wall commemorating her life.

Despite the pain and degradation of slavery, the grueling hardship of two pioneer treks across the wilderness and the difficulties of illiteracy, Biddy chose to spend each day in Christlike service to others. The ultimate manifestation of her charitable spirit is demonstrated by her choices after she was emancipated. Biddy's life is an example of the Savior's words in Matthew 25:34–36: "Come, ye blessed of my Father, inherit the kingdom prepared for you from the foundation of the world: For I was an hungered, and

ye gave me meat: I was thirsty, and ye gave me drink: I was a stranger, and ye took me in: Naked, and ye clothed me: I was sick, and ye visited me: I was in prison, and ye came unto me." Every blessing she received she used again to help someone in need. Her faith and devotion to her Father in Heaven shine through the murky waters of a time when equality and freedom were more of a dream than a reality. Biddy served women of all races and social distinctions, helping them bring new life into the world. She offered the gift and power of literacy to others, when she herself was denied it. Unable to record her own story, her legacy is written instead in the lives of all she lifted up, fed, and strengthened. She used her hard-earned prosperity to rescue those in the midst of the same poverty and abuse from which she arose. Her true heart is found in words she frequently shared with others as quoted by her great-granddaughter, Gladys Owens Smith, "*If you hold your hand closed, . . . nothing good can come in. The open hand is blessed, for it gives in abundance, even as it receives.*"[18]

NOTES

1.   Dolores Hayden, "Biddy Mason: Los Angeles 1856–1891," *California History* 68, no. 3 (Fall 1989): 86–99.

2.   Ibid., 88.

3.   De Etta Demaratus, *The Force of a Feather: The Seearch for a Lost Story of Slavery and Freedom* (Salt Lake City: University of Utah Press, 2002).

4.   "Biddy Mason: Los Angeles 1856–1891," 88.

5.   Edith Klemke and Bob Weed. *Robert Mays Smith: From South Carolina to Texas (the Long Way)* (Wolfe City, TX: Hennington, 1998).

6.   "Biddy Mason: Los Angeles 1856–1891," 89–90.

7.   Ibid., 89.

8.   Ibid., 90.

9.   Ibid., 91.

10.   Ibid., 92.

11.   Ibid., 93.

12.   Ibid., 95, 99.

13.   Ibid., 97.

14.   Ibid., 99.

15.   Ibid., 93.

16.   Ibid., 97.

17.   Ibid., 98.

18.   Ibid., 99.

ZINA DIANTHA
HUNTINGTON YOUNG

January 31, 1821–August 8, 1901

"O how little we know what a day may bring forth.
Prepare me to stand all things."[1]

MUCH OF WHAT WE KNOW ABOUT THIS remarkable woman comes from Zina's own hand. She kept a daily journal, chronicling her life, her spiritual learning, and the activity of the Saints and the Church. From her writings, we gain an intimate understanding of the sorrows and triumphs of early Church pioneers. This historical treasure was discovered some years ago in a descendant's locked trunk.

Zina Diantha Huntington Young was born in Watertown, Ontario County, New York, on January 31, 1821, to William and Zina Huntington. The Huntington family forsook their prosperous farm to journey to Kirtland in 1836, after their hearts received the message of the restored gospel.[2] Zina was baptized by Hyrum Smith. She loved to sing and was a member of the Mormon Temple Choir. Zina was introduced to the art of nursing

9

by following her mother around the city as she tended to the sick and afflicted. Newly a woman herself and very impressionable, Zina learned at the hand of her mother valuable lessons about the gift of new life and how to ease suffering. Peace and prosperity were short-lived, as the persecutions of the Saints began to rage all around. The family moved with their remnants and scattered belongings to Nauvoo. Her mother passed away during these struggles, leaving Zina to care for the household.[3]

After a few years, Zina married Henry Bailey Jacobs on March 7, 1841.[4] They were blessed with a son, Zebulon William, one year later. Some sources describe their marriage as unhappy, but Zina never disparages their relationship in her writings. Henry served several missions for the Church and was often away. Henry gave his blessing for Zina to be sealed to Joseph Smith on October 27, 1841.[5] We are unsure of the details of these early sealings and how they affected temporal relationships, and Zina does not record her most sacred experiences on paper. We do feel her keen sorrow when news of the martyrdom reaches Nauvoo.

"Thus in one day about 3 or 4 oclock fell the Prophet and Patriarch of the Church of Latterday Saints, the kind husbands, the affectionate Father, the venerable statesman, the friends of man kinde, by the hand of a ruthless Mob mixed with desenters. O God how long before thou wilt avenge the innocent blood that has be[e]n shed?"[6]

A time of confusion followed the martyrdom of Joseph Smith. Zina speaks of the succession of Brigham Young and the unity of the Saints when faced with threatening mobs.

"The church is in prosperous circumstances for there appears to be the most union there has ever ben [sic]. The faithful are determined to keep the law of God. O Father bind us as a people together in the bonds of love that we never shall separate."[7]

All the while, her daily entries describe her ministry to the sick and those with child. Her skills as a practitioner grew through trial and error and sage advice from compatriot Patty Sessions, a respected and experienced midwife. In her diary, Zina is always quick to give gratitude to Heavenly Father for the blessing of healing. She, along with the other Saints, continued to labor hard to finish the temple, despite the mobs and their murderous intent. With great joy she relates the completion of the Nauvoo Temple.

"The last stone was lade on the Temple with shouts of Hosanah [sic] to God and the Lamb, amen &c. Joy filled every bosom and thanks to our God that had preserved us."[8]

As the Saints fled Nauvoo, Zina, great with child, felt the pains of labor coming on strongly. She bore a second son, Henry Chariton, on the frozen banks of the Chariton River in Iowa. A few hours later, the group of Saints continued their flight with Zina lying on a makeshift bed atop wooden barrels in the back of a wagon. The hardest time of Zina's life was yet to come, however.

Encamped at Mount Pisgah, her husband left her with her two young boys to return to the States. He grew weary of the persecution and lost his testimony. Alone and unsure of the future, with little food, Zina returned to her father William's household. The family struggled through the winter with scant provisions and poor shelter. Her father weakened in health and passed away despite Zina's ministrations. Brigham Young, seeing her plight, extended her an offer to join his household at Winter Quarters, which she gladly accepted. She worked hard to relieve the suffering of the people during this time, her experiences with sorrow giving her greater compassion for those in distress. Susa Young Gates wrote of her, "In no other line of work and effort was Aunt Zina better known and more appreciated than in her ministrations to the sick and dying in the household of faith. She was an angel of hope and faith to thousands and thousands of the Latter-day Saints. Who has not seen the heavenly comfort and faith beaming from her eye as she knelt over the sick or soothed the mourner!"[9]

Zina reached the Salt Lake Valley in 1848 at age twenty-seven. The large Young family lived in tents while the fort was being constructed.[10] Brigham soon built a separate, humble adobe house. The inside was tastefully furnished with Brigham's hand-carved furniture. It is in this new dwelling that Brigham and Zina have their only child together, a daughter born in 1850 and named for her mother and grandmother. Brigham noticed Zina's raw intelligence and encouraged her to study obstetrics more. She received additional training under the hand of Dr. Mary Barker, a traveling physician.[11] Zina would become midwife to nearly all of Brigham's children and hundreds of others in the community. We see in Zina's actions her true feelings for her patients. When a patient, Clarissa Ross died in childbirth, Zina took her four young children and raised them as her own.[12]

Zina also knew when to call for additional help. When attending the birth of her son Chariton's first child, Zina recognized that the birth was not progressing normally. She had Chariton send for the doctor. He protested, thinking Zina's skills equal to the task. She again insisted, and he went for the doctor. The infant was delivered with forceps and the tiny darkened baby lay limp on the bed. While the doctor worked hard to help

Emma, Zina began to resuscitate the baby with a time-honored technique. Soon a tiny cry gladdened the hearts of those present. Zina's humility and quick action saved two lives that day.

Zina served in many other areas as well. She was president of the Utah Silk Association, a difficult calling that required her to overcome a deep loathing of worms.[13] She worked hard in the suffrage movement and represented the women of Utah in the 1893 Chicago World's Fair. Her missionary work led her to the Sandwich Islands.[14] Her most important work, besides bringing babies into the world, was her service as general Relief Society president, succeeding her best friend, Eliza Roxcy Snow.[15] Zina passed away on August 8, 1901, shortly after visiting her daughter in Canada. Her life is summarized sweetly in her tribute published in the *Relief Society Magazine*: "There have been many noble women, some great women, and a multitude of good women, associated, past and present, with the Latter-day work. But of them all, none was so lovely, so lovable, and so greatly beloved as was 'Aunt Zina.'"[16]

NOTES

1. *Zina Diantha Huntington Young Diary 1844–1847*, typescript, Church Archives, The Church of Jesus Christ of Latter-day Saints, Salt Lake City, Utah, 310.

2. Susa Young Gates, *History of the Young Ladies' Mutual Improvement Association of the Church of Jesus Christ of Latter-day Saints from November 1869 to June 1910* (Salt Lake City: *Deseret News*, 1911), in "Centennial of President Zina D. H. Young," *Relief Society Magazine* 8, no. 3 (March 1921), 133.

3. Barbara B. Smith and Blythe Darlyn Thatcher, eds. "This Is the Truth, Truth, Truth!" in *Heroines of the Restoration*. (Salt Lake City: Bookcraft, 1997), 118.

4. Ibid.

5. Maureen Ursenbach Beecher, "'All Things move in Order in the City': the Nauvoo Diary of Zina Diantha Huntington Jacobs," *BYU Studies Quarterly* 19, no. 3 (Provo, UT: Brigham Young University Press, 1979), 288.

6. *Zina Diantha Huntington Young Diary*, 292.

7. Ibid., 305.

8. Ibid., 311.

9. "Centennial of President Zina D. H. Young," *Relief Society Magazine* 8, no. 3 (March 1921), 133.

10. "All Things Move in Order in the City," 288.

11. "Centennial of President Zina D. H. Young," 133.

12. "This Is the Truth, Truth, Truth!" 121.

13. "This Is the Truth, Truth, Truth!" 122; "Centennial of President Zina D. H. Young,"133.

14. "Centennial of President Zina D. H. Young," 133–34.

15. "This Is the Truth, Truth, Truth!" 123; "Centennial of President Zina D. H. Young," 133.

16. "Centennial of President Zina D. H. Young," 130.

MARY HEATHMAN SMITH

(January 21, 1818–December 17, 1895)

Mary Heathman Smith was an educated and refined mother of ten children, who served those who lived in the Ogden Valley for over twenty-five years. Known as "Grandma Smith," she brought over 1,500 babies into the local pioneer communities.

ARY WAS BORN TO SUCCESSFUL ENGLISH farmers, Isaac and Elizabeth, in the winter of 1818. She grew strong helping with farm chores. Due to her parents' hard work and frugality, Mary was able to attend national school until age sixteen. At this time, the course of her life would be changed forever. Her generous father had secured a bond for a friend in the amount of $20,000. When this friend was unable to pay, Isaac was then forced to sell his home and thriving farm to repay the debt.[1] The family moved to Oxton, where Elizabeth obtained employment as a servant to a titled lady. In a stroke of good fortune, her father was appointed by the king to be the collector of customs at the port of Liverpool. Mary was able to begin training at a maternity hospital in the area and excelled in her studies. This knowledge would serve her throughout her entire life. Three years later, she met and married a stonemason, John A. Smith, on April 29, 1840.[2] Mary spent this time as a wife and nurse. After five years, they were blessed with their first child, Julia. Mary Ann came a year later, but she died soon after birth. By 1850, the family included Isaac, Thomas, and William George. In this same year the first taste of the gospel came to John and Mary. Their hearts readily

received the message of the Restoration preached by the missionaries, and they were soon members of the fledgling Birkenhead Branch of the Church.[3] The next eleven years brought growth in the gospel and five additional children: May Ann, Joseph, Elizabeth, John, and Matilda. Mary was forty-two years old when she delivered Matilda. Excited by the prospect of gathering with the Saints in Utah, John decided to leave for America in May of 1861. The call to Zion was strong, but he needed to go ahead of the family and work to earn the funds bring them later.[4]

Mary took employment with Dr. Gordon, who, after observing her medical skills, paid her a good wage. She saved every penny, supporting her nine children by herself. John wrote to his wife that he loved his new land. Mary replied that she was coming immediately over on the next ship. Mary and her nine children set sail for America in May 1862. Five weeks of rough seas brought the sickened and weak family to New York, where they stayed for two weeks to regain their health.[5] They traveled by rail and boat to Winter Quarters, Nebraska, and joined the wagon train of sixty led by Henry H. Miller.[6] Edward Rishton drove the team that brought Mary and her family one thousand miles to Zion. Along the path, he spoke lovingly of his home in Huntsville and may have influenced the family to move there two years after their arrival in the Salt Lake Valley.[7] He spoke of the tall majestic mountains and green valleys with virgin soil ready for cultivation. Mary may have been eager to escape the coal-blackened streets of Britain and return to the country.

Mary helped the sick and afflicted and maintained a busy midwifery practice in Huntsville. She was the only person in the Ogden Valley with training to set broken bones, suture wounds, and handle difficult obstetric cases. Mary charged three dollars for ten days' care if the family could afford to pay,[8] and nothing if they were impoverished. Often, the families she ministered to would share their wood or produce instead of money. She was a grandmother by this time and was known as "Old Lady Smith" or "Granny Smith."

Many adversities graced the lives of Mary and her family. John was brought home after an encounter with a grizzly bear, and only the quick and able suturing skills of Mary prevented the loss of his leg, and potentially his life, from blood loss and infection.[9] His wound healed quickly, and he returned to work a few weeks later. The Smiths' oldest daughter, Julia, married Benjamin Bowen in 1863. They were called to settle Toquerville. After ten years of marriage, she wished to return home to Huntsville. Julia's son Thomas was injured on the return journey when his gun accidentally

discharged.[10] He was delivered to Mary's threshold, clinging to life. Mary knew when a condition required expertise beyond her own. The closest doctor advised amputation, but even this brought only a small chance of survival. Thomas refused the procedure, and Mary held her grandson close to her breast as his young life slipped away.

Mary's daughter Elizabeth followed in her mother's footsteps and became an avid and compassionate midwife. In her declining years, Elizabeth was able to relieve a great deal of Mary's duties. As she lay on her deathbed, Mary made a special request of Bishop David McKay. She asked for the church bells to toll as her casket was carried forth, as was the practice in her native land. She wished for a bouquet of wheat to be placed on her casket to symbolize that she had lived to a ripe age and was ready to be buried and "spring forth" as new tender plants on the morn of the Resurrection. Above all, she wished to be buried in the grave of her sweetheart, John, who had died twenty-three years earlier. [11]

Mary gave her essence to her family, her community, her church, and her God. In the twenty-five years she practiced in the Ogden Valley area, she delivered over fifteen hundred babies. "Grandma Smith" was a convert, immigrant, pioneer, healer, loving wife and mother of ten children, and respected midwife in her new mountain home. [12]

NOTES

1.   Smith, William G. *Biographical Sketch of Mary Heathman Smith*, compiled by Carol Widdison, submitted to International Society of Daughters of Utah Pioneers, April 1991, 1.

2.   Ibid.

3.   Ibid.

4.   Ibid.

5.   Ibid.

6.   Ibid., 2.

7.   Ibid.

8.   Ibid., 2–3.

9.   Ibid., 3.

10. Ibid., 5.

11. Ibid, 3.

12. Ibid., 2.

NETTA ANNA FURRER CARDON

March 15, 1826–August 15, 1907

*Stalwart convert, handcart pioneer,
compassionate physician, faithful mother*

NETTA ANNA FURRER CARDON WAS BORN ON a small farm in Pfibacon Canton, Zurich, Switzerland, on March 15, 1826, to a family of six children.[1] Her parents strongly believed in education, and Netta was fortunate to attend school from the age of five. As she grew, her intelligence was noted. At the age of four-teen, she asked to study nursing and was sent to Lamples Hospital for a four-year course. She was encouraged to study to become a physician by her cousin David Eptner, a professor of medicine at Geneva Hospital. She began her courses and studied hard. Meanwhile, unbeknownst to her, her father and brother were killed in combat. Her mother wished to spare her the distraction of sorrow, and this tragic news did not reach her until after her graduation as a physician and

surgeon.[2] She returned home to care for and subsequently bury her mother, who never rose out of her grief.

Perhaps these losses prepared her heart to receive the message that Elders Smith and Heurs preached to her in 1854. Only Netta received the glad tidings of the restored gospel. Her family remained staunchly opposed to her new faith and forbade her to emigrate to Utah. Netta Anna knew her course. Gathering her small inheritance from her parents' estate, she boarded the ship *Enoch's Train* under an assumed name and set sail for America. "Doctor Anna" was instrumental in saving many lives during the difficult crossing.[3]

She soon found herself on the banks on the Missouri River, new wagon and strong team ready, her Swiss treasures safely stowed behind her. Seeing a large family without the money to purchase a team, she gave them hers. Her treasures, which she had carried across an ocean, she divided amongst those gathered. She bought a handcart and loaded her medical bag, a blue silk dress, and a few provisions, and began the trek across the plains in the Edmund Ellsworth Handcart Company.[4] She walked barefoot most of the way. A granddaughter, Mary Anna Shaw Bjorkman, recalls:

> A particular incident in which Miss Furrer acted the important part was a case of two young boys who were seriously sick, not expecting them to live and the company being so near destitution and starvation, they left the two boys for whom they could see no hope, to meet their fate, as others before them had certainly met theirs. The parents of these boys had met death from lack of food. From the time these two boys had been left to perish by the wayside, Anna's heart had not been at ease. Her thoughts had been with those suffering children, and after they had gone several miles past them, she determined to go back for the sufferers. The persuasions of the company could not convince her that she should not go back to the dying boys. When she arrived where the boys were she was thirty miles behind the company. She pulled the handcart with the additional load of those two boys the remainder of the journey. Extra exertion was necessary to rejoin the company. She continued [as] savior to these two boys, sharing her two tablespoons of flour with them daily until their arrival in Salt Lake. The boys thus saved by Miss Furrer lived to grow to manhood and afterward resided in Provo.[5]

Upon her arrival in the valley, Netta Anna met her future husband, John Cardon, through Brigham Young. After marrying in 1856, they moved to Big Cottonwood and then to Weber County. In addition to her busy practice, she and John built the first carding mill and later opened a

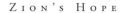

general store in Ogden. They were blessed with six children, though three went to early graves.[6]

Netta Anna's life was spent helping others. Brigham Young had counseled her to "use her medical knowledge in helping the sick and needy without remuneration and great would be her blessings."[7] She set broken bones, delivered babies, tended wounds and burns and cared for the ill. She traveled by horse, often in the middle of the night. She tended herself at the births of her own children. She saved carefully and purchased the first piano in Weber County, and Eliza R. Snow came up to give her daughter Rozina lessons. Netta Anna was known for her surgical skills and compassion for the destitute. Indeed, we see this in her first acts as a new pioneer as she gave away all she had to help the hurting, and as she nursed two forsaken boys back to health. "Doctor Anna" left a legacy of skill and generosity to those she served.

NOTES

1. Anna Hermina Shaw. "History of My Mother: Netta Anna Furrer Cardon," compiled by Isabelle E. K. Wilson, Daughters of Utah Pioneers, collected and filed 1963.

2. Daniel Drumiler, *Anna Regula Furrer, Life History*. Presented August 9, 1997, Philippe Cardon Reunion.

3. Ibid.

4. "History of My Mother: Netta Anna Furrer Cardon."

5. Notes taken from the journal of Anna Hermina Shaw Bjorkman.

6. "History of My Mother: Netta Anna Furrer Cardon."

7. Ibid.

MARY JANE
McCLEVE MEEKS

August 21, 1840–January 19, 1933

*Mother of ten, midwife in Orderville who brought over
seven hundred babies into the world, generous servant.*

MARY JANE McCLEVE MEEKS WAS BORN ON
August 21, 1840, in Belfast, Ireland, as one of ten children
of John and Nancy Jane McCleve. Her father was a shoe-
maker, and her mother was a seamstress. Mary's mother was the first of the
family to accept the restored gospel and was baptized, though her father
opposed it, in June 1841. However, John joined the Church four years later.
When Mary was eight, because of staunch opposition to the Church, she
was baptized at night in the Irish Sea by Elder Robert Wallace. Later, when
Mary was fourteen, the McCleve family, desiring to gather with the Saints
in America, saved their money and sent the oldest daughters, Sarah and
Catherine, to the United States in 1854, following by sea two years later
on the ship *Enoch's Train*. The family traveled from Liverpool, England,
to Boston, Massachusetts, where they traveled by rail to Iowa City, Iowa.[1]
From Iowa, they began their journey west in the second handcart company
captained by Daniel McArthur.[2]

The descendants of Mary describe her as having a small "strong body,"
with dark hair pulled back into a neat bun at the nape of her neck. She
had "a witty tongue" and "her sympathetic understanding and her Irish
wit made her popular with her traveling companions."[3] She helped pull the

heavy cart and would sometimes carry her youngest brother, John, and even other travelers' children as needed.[4] Dangers stalked the struggling company on the road west. Mary was once nearly abducted by several men of ill repute hiding on the riverbank where she went to wash the family laundry. Rattlesnakes, hunger, and sickness besieged the company. Her father, John, "couldn't eat when he knew his children were hungry, so he divided his scanty portion [of rations] with them."[5] He died two days before reaching the valley and is buried in an unmarked grave in Echo Canyon. John's sacrifice helped shape Mary's character and inspire her constant generosity toward those in need.

Upon arrival in the Salt Lake Valley, the family was treated to "banquets of delicious food and comfortable, clean beds" and was finally reunited with Mary and Catherine, which was "best of all."[6] Mary found employment with the Gifford family and worked hard for "one yard of calico per week"[7] to make a dress. She was well liked by the Giffords, and both of their sons desired her hand in marriage. It was at this time that she became acquainted with and desired to marry Dr. Pridday Meeks, who was forty-five years her senior, whom she had "seen . . . in a dream."[8] She was sealed to Dr. Meeks on November 12, 1856. Dr. Meek's other wife Sarah and her three daughters welcomed Mary Jane. Mary Jane spoke of their relationship as a warm friendship. Mary and Pridday welcomed ten children into the world, the last being born when Pridday was eighty-two years old.[9] In addition to his medical practice, Dr. Meeks also farmed new settlements in Parowan, Berryville (Glendale), and Harrisburg. Mary knew the pangs of loss, enduring the deaths of two-week-old John from infection and nineteen-month-old Charles from burns.[10] In 1877, the Meeks family moved to Orderville, where they would spend the rest of their lives. It was here that Mary began to serve as a midwife in the local community. Her husband gave her some instruction and Mary answered a call that she would have great talents for.[11] Mary was a devoted and hardworking mother and midwife. According to her daughter Ellen, Mary "brought seven hundred babies into the world without losing a mother or baby in more than twenty years of practice. She always believed in going the second mile. She was on call day and night. She not only delivered the babies and made the Mother comfortable but frequently cared for the family for ten days. . . . One time she came home minus her petticoat. 'I gave it away . . . The poor sister had none so I gave her mine.' Another time she came home in her stocking feet. 'Oh I gave them to Sister —, she had none and I knew I had another pair at home.'"[12]

Mary Jane was "friendly [and] outgoing. She gave freely of herself as

long as she lived. She loved people and took long walks every day to visit friends and neighbors."[13] She also had a wonderful sense of humor. When she was eighty-three, she went to visit a granddaughter, Ida Balken, in Salt Lake City. She explained, *"My darling, when I came pulling a handcart into this valley, I little dreamed that I would live to see the day when people would come flying in here through the air."*[14]

Another granddaughter, Lourie Meeks Morrill, remarks, "I remember my Grandmother Meeks as a little, energetic woman, slender and straight as an arrow. . . . Grandma never wasted anything. Hunger had been too real to her. The only time I remember grandma getting after me was when I wasted a slice of bread. . . . The greatest gift of all was her devotion and the heritage she passed on to us."[15]

Mary Jane embraced the joys and sorrows of this life and clung to the gospel with all her might. At the age of ninety, she remarked, *"I used to think I would be content to live until my family was raised; now I would like to see my grandchildren grown-up. There just isn't any stopping place."*[16] At her death, her posterity numbered seven living children, sixty-two grandchildren, one hundred thirty-one great-grandchildren and fifteen great-great grandchildren.[17]

NOTES

1. Lourie Meeks Morrill, *Biography of Mary Jane McCleave Meeks*, collected for Daughter of Utah Pioneers, filed December 1960, 1.

2. Claire Noall, "Mormon Midwives," *Utah Historical Quarterly* 10 (1942), 125.

3. *Biography of Mary Jane McCleave Meeks*, 1.

4. Ibid.

5. Ibid., 2.

6. Ibid.

7. "Mormon Midwives," 127.

8. *Biography of Mary Jane McCleave Meeks*, 2.

9. Ibid., 2–3

10. Ibid., 3.

11. "Mormon Midwives,"126.

12. *Biography of Mary Jane McCleave Meeks*, 4.

13. Ibid.

14. "Mormon Midwives," 127.

15. Ibid., 3.

16. Ibid., 4.

17. *Biography of Mary Jane McCleave Meeks*, 5.

PHEBE AMELIA
RICHARDS PEART

June 7, 1851–January 15, 1943

Pursued her calling despite negative pressures in the outside world,
mother of seven, said to have had the gift of healing in her touch

PHEBE WAS BORN TO MARY THOMPSON AND Dr. Willard Richards in June of 1851. A strong girl and natural beauty, she had long dark curls, rosy cheeks, and a regal posture. She was referred to as the "black-eyed beauty." Phebe showed an eagerness and natural aptitude for medicine. She began tending to the sick at age fourteen, but it was while helping at a birth that she first felt inside the call of her heart. Her daughter Amelia writes, "When she was on her first call, she decided that some day she would be a midwife. Being aware of the prejudice that existed against the services of men doctors for women in confinement, and knowing how greatly midwives were needed, she looked forward to the day when she could study for this profession."[1] Phebe had several strikes against her realization of this dream: her father had passed away and the large family was destitute. She was also very young, and her mother strongly desired her to marry and give up her career aspirations.[2] Phebe knew what it was to go hungry, having spoken of her youth, "*I was so hungry I would have eaten a worm, if I could have found a worm.*"[3] She continued to learn on the side, while working hard to bring food to her family. Four years later, she was joined in marriage to Jacob Peart Jr., who had strong convictions about how Phebe should spend her life—in the home. When she asked his and

her mother's "permission and their help in taking a course of study under Dr. [Ellis] Shipp . . . both . . . were bitterly opposed to the suggestion." Phebe knew that she had been given both the desire to serve women and the talent for a reason. She quietly pled her case before the Stake Relief Society Presidency, who agreed to fund her studies. Her daughter Amelia relates, "The Relief Society was sympathetic to her desire, and through it, even in the face of dire opposition at home, Phebe eventually completed her training and received from Dr. Shipp a certificate which made her eligible to practice nursing and obstetrics."[4]

Phebe loved practicing in her new calling, traveling all over the Farmington area to deliver and care for women. She was no stranger to birth, having brought seven children of her own into the world. When she was called to a difficult case, she would call on her brothers, Dr. Joseph Richards and Dr. Stephen Richards, for support and advice. [5]

"Aunt Phebe" was always near if called on and gave the majority of her service for free, in gratitude for the help she had received in her education. She was superb at her ministrations. Amelia explains,

> Rare indeed was loss of life under the watchful eye and patient administration of this good woman. She was said to have had the gift of healing in her touch. Many patients insisted that they drew strength from her strong healthy body while she massaged them. . . . The babies that she brought into the world number hundreds. In those days it was not uncommon for the midwife or nurse to do all of the housework, the cooking and washing for the entire family, and to keep an eye on the smaller members of the brood, while all the time she was caring for the mother and newborn babe. But having been blessed with a physique that was exceptional in its strength and endurance, Phebe considered no task too great to surmount. Hard labor and loss of sleep were taken in stride.[6]

Phebe spent her life fulfilling the calling placed in her heart and mothering her children. She worked in the Salt Lake Temple for over twenty years.[7] She remained active even at the closure of her life. At the age of ninety-one, "the urge to nurse the sick [was] still strong." She would say: *"Oh, I wish I could get in and nurse as I used to do. I'm sure I could straighten you up in no time, but I haven't the strength any more."*[8]

NOTES

1. Amelia Peart Macdonald, *Life Sketch of my Mother, Phebe Amelia Richards Peart*. Filed with Daughters of Utah Pioneers, 1960. Also published in Claire Noall, "Mormon Midwives," *Utah Historical Quarterly* 10 (1942), 117.

2. Claire Noall, "Mormon Midwives," *Utah Historical Quarterly* 10 (1942), 117.

3. *Deseret News* Obituary, January 16, 1943.

4. "Mormon Midwives," 117.

5. Ibid.

6. *Life Sketch of my Mother, Phebe Amelia Richards Peart*; "Mormon Midwives," 117–18.

7. *Deseret News* Obituary, January 16, 1943.

8. *Life Sketch of my Mother, Phebe Amelia Richards Peart*; "Mormon Midwives," 119.

SARAH HEALD GREENHALGH

November 27, 1827–January 14, 1922

*Midwife and nurse capable of meeting
any situation with courage and faith*[1]

ONE OF THE BEST-KNOWN PIONEER MIDWIVES, Sarah was born far away in Lancashire, England, on November 7, 1827. She and her husband would find the Church there and make the decision to come to America in 1854, when Sarah was twenty-seven and a young mother. While at sea, her infant daughter died and was buried. Her granddaughter Genevieve writes how "sometimes, in the midst of her family, she would tell how nearly her heart was broken when the body of one of her babies, strapped to a weighted board, was lowered into the sea from the sailing vessel on which she was crossing to America."[2]

The family was asked to move to Bear Lake County in 1865. Sarah was then a mother of seven. She was called as a midwife at this time, though she had no formal training. She was told that God would bless her and magnify her work. This new wild country had no doctors, but she grew into the task as she "had the job to do."[3] Her territory included families from Montpelier, Fish Haven, and Laketown nearly one hundred miles altogether. She worked alongside Annie Bryceon Laker, a personal friend, and taught the other midwives of the area, including Orissa Allred, Sister Bridges (Montpelier), Sister Sparks (Dingle), Emmeline Rich, and Sister Findlay (Paris).[4] Sarah was known also for her gift of song. She was asked to sing at town

gatherings for over forty years. Some of her favorite songs included "Bell Brandon," and "The Rain."[5]

Sarah was known for her efficiency and charity. Her house was highly organized, which allowed her the freedom to care for others, without neglecting her own family. She was industrious and would work hard each day to accomplish her tasks. Her granddaughter Genvieve writes:

> Well-cooked meals were served on an exact schedule. Every day had its specific routine, which was cared for by the children when Grandma was away. . . . Often she was paid for her services in produce, although much of her work was done as charity, because food was scarce and money was almost a minus quantity. She was called from her home hundreds of times to wash and lay out the dead. On many an occasion, after cooking a good meal for her large family, she would hear a knock at the door before she herself was seated at the table. Sometimes, in answer to the knock, she would be gone a week or more, depending on the nature of the case to which she had been called. . . . Long after other midwives and doctors located in Bear Lake County, her services were sought because of her unusual success. I remember her as a calm, reserved, yet forceful character, capable of meeting any situation with courage and faith.[6]

Part of Sarah's loving and responsible care came out of her own sorrows in the loss of her infant at sea and later the untimely death of her forty-three-year-old daughter, who left behind ten children. She spoke over her daughter as she was laid out in the casket, "'My baby, . . . how could I know that I would bury you?' . . . She put her arms around her child and kissed her," then rose and steeled herself for what lay next.[7] It is this same fortitude that enabled her to raise ten children and serve her community in their times of joy and sorrow. She was greatly loved and respected for her work and nobility of bearing. She died at the age of ninety-five, in her home in Bloomington, Idaho.[8]

NOTES

1. Genevieve Wilcox, "Interview," in *Utah Historical Quarterly* 10 (1942), 124.
2. Franklin Greenhalgh, "Letter," in *Utah Historical Quarterly* 10 (1942), 123.
3. *Utah Historical Quarterly* 10 (1942), 123.
4. Ibid., 122–23.
5. Genevieve Wilcox, "Interview," in *Utah Historical Quarterly* 10 (1942), 124.
6. Ibid.
7. Ibid.
8. Ibid.

HARRIET SANDERS KIMBALL

December 7, 1824–September 5, 1868

*Faithful convert, survivor, mother, and caring nurse
and midwife to the poor*

HARRIET SANDERS (NE HELGA YSTEINSDATTER Bakka) was born in Atraa, Norway, on December 7, 1824, to Ystein and Aase Bakka. She, along with her two brothers and four sisters, came to America in August 1837, when Harriet was ten, in the hope of finding a better life in a new land. They settled in Indiana and began tilling the soil. Sadly, both parents died of typhoid fever within several weeks of each other. The orphaned children struggled to keep the family together and farm the land. Out of necessity, they were scattered and had to live with other families. In 1842, Harriet and her sister Ellen were moved to La Salle County, Illinois, where several other Norwegian families were homesteading. Elder George P. Dykes came into the area with news of the restoration. The gospel first reached the ears of Harriet, Ellen, and their brother Sondra at this time, and their hearts were ready

to hear the news that they could be reunited with their dear parents again.[1]
Hope had come to them out of great loss. After being baptized, they moved
to Nauvoo. She became a guest in the Joseph Young home and was introduced to Emmeline B. Wells, who became a lifelong friend to Harriet. She
and her sister Ellen were joined in marriage to Heber Chase Kimball on
January 7, 1846, just days prior to the flight of the Saints from Nauvoo
due to severe persecution. Harriet came to Utah in the Heber C. Kimball
Company in 1848. The Kimball family lived in Salt Lake City and assisted
in the work of leading the Church. During this time Harriet also gave birth
to three children: Harriet, Hyrum, and Eugene. She became well known in
the area for her kind ministrations to the sick and those with child. She was
known as the "Kimball family doctor" because of her "exceptional power
of healing and her natural talent for nursing."[2] According to records of the
time, she brought over five hundred babies into the world. After Heber's
death in 1868, Harriet and her sister Ellen desired a change. The two sisters, along with eleven Kimball sons, moved to the small mountain community of Meadowville, near the Bear Lake Valley, reminiscent of her long
forgotten Nordic land. Harriet continued to work hard, taming the wilderness and serving others with all her heart. She was "loved and admired," and
was someone who people "turned to in times of sickness and trouble, a great
friend to all."[3] Harriet died on September 5, 1868, at home. Despite her
struggles in a land far from her birth—the pain of losing her parents, the
persecution of the mobs, widowhood—Harriet showed unwavering faith in
what she believed.

NOTES

1. Aagot Kimball, (Ellen) Sanders Kimball, 1–2, http://xmission
.com~rhubarb/bcrk-ellen.htm. (Website no longer available.) The sisters have an
intertwined history.

2. Pat M. Geisler. *Women of Faith and Fortitude: Harriet Sanders Kimball.*
Heber C. Kimball Family Association, archived by Daughter of Utah Pioneers.
1976, 1.

3. Ibid.

CATHERINE MARY MEICKLEJOHN TODD OLDROYD

August 4, 1822–April 1, 1897

Convert, Scottish immigrant, mother of ten, midwife of 1,400, pioneer of Ephraim and Manti

C**ATHERINE MARY WAS BORN IN THE HIGH**lands of Scotland on August 4, 1822. We know little of her humble beginnings but much of her adult adventures. At age 18, she married Andrew Todd in Glasgow, Scotland.[1] They were quickly blessed with children, a daughter and two sons. Sadly, their son, John, died soon after birth. In 1846, her husband unexpectedly died. She was four months along with their fourth child. Catherine's heart would soon break again as her precious daughter and infant passed away in 1847. With only young Archibald left, Catherine was left to heal from her grief and find a way to support herself and her son.

In this crucible of pain, the soothing truths of the gospel filled Catherine with

hope again. She was baptized on August 7, 1848. In 1850, she met and married Peter Liddle Oldroyd, also a member of the Church.[2] A son, William, was born in Glasgow in 1850, but again died shortly after birth. The couple adopted a baby girl named Janet, who had been born at the same time as little William, but she would pass away at ten months. Catherine's arms ached for the children she continually bore and watched slip away. These feelings would drive her to become a careful and empathetic midwife.

The young family decided to emigrate to Utah and soon braved the difficult crossing on the ship *Falcon*. Upon reaching the Missouri staging point, they joined Appleton Harmon's company and crossed the plains, arriving in Salt Lake in 1852. They first settled in Cherry (now Centerville), but stayed only a brief time. Later in the year, they were called to go to Manti, and then on to Ephraim in 1853. She was the first white woman to live in the fort there. They worked this wild land for ten years and then answered a call to the Sevier Valley during troubled times. Young Catherine was in hostile Indian territory during the Black Hawk War, with five young children, being called and set apart to serve as midwife and nurse for the area. Most women would have shied away from an arduous task for which they had no training other than that which nature had brought them through experience. But Catherine said yes.[3] Blessed are the 1,400 or more children she subsequently helped guide into the world,[4] and the countless sick and injured who found relief under her capable hands. When the Sevier settlements were abandoned, the family moved to Fountain Green, where Catherine continued her midwifery practice and also served as a Counselor in the Relief Society presidency, as well as a teacher. In the happy laughter of her thriving children, Catherine found a balm of peace after so much heartache.[5] She peacefully passed away on April 1, 1897, with the sure knowledge that six children waited to rush into her arms on the other side. She left a legacy of service, devotion, and faith in the midst of despair.[6] According to her obituary given in the *Deseret News* on April 10, 1897, "she was much respected and beloved by all who knew her, and always has been a faithful member of the Church."[7]

NOTES

1.   Pat M. Geisler, *Women of Faith and Fortitude: Catherine Mary Meicklejohn Todd Oldroyd*, archived by Daughters of Utah Pioneers, November 3, 2004.

2.   Ibid.

3.   *Deseret News*, "Obituary of Catherine Mary Oldroyd," April 10, 1897.

4. *Women of Faith and Fortitude: Catherine Mary Meicklejohn Todd Oldroyd.*
5. "Obituary of Catherine Mary Oldroyd."
6. *Women of Faith and Fortitude: Catherine Mary Meicklejohn Todd Oldroyd.*
7. "Obituary of Catherine Mary Oldroyd."

SARAH ZURVIAH
SOUTHWORTH BURBANK

February 10, 1835–May 28, 1927

"I came to this earth to attend the sick. I have prayed for my parents who were very sick and they have recovered. When I have been in confinement cases the Lord has blessed me in delivering women when they were in a very serious condition."[1]

SARAH ZURVIAH SOUTHWORTH BURBANK WAS born on February 10, 1835, in Boston, Ontario, Canada, to Chester Southworth and Mary Byington. As a young girl she helped her father with farming chores. The family joined the Church, sold all they owned, and moved to the United States to join the Saints in Kirtland, Ohio. From Kirtland, they made the exodus to Missouri. They were sent to Far West, Missouri, and were driven out in the cold of winter, temporarily finding refuge in Nauvoo. The Saints were in the midst of turmoil following the death of Joseph Smith and the persecution of the mobs. They fled across the river to Iowa,[2] where Sarah's young sister died and had to be buried along the way. Sarah records in her journal:

> We were driven from Kirtland to Far West, Missouri and again to Caldwell and from there to Montrose Illinois and later to Nauvoo, and later from Nauvoo. The only direction we had left to flee was West! In this flight we had to cross the Mississippi river in the night on a flat bottomed boat to save our lives. The people were camped by the river, some of which were without tents and some sick and some dying. We did not know where we were going

but got word . . . we were going a way out West. . . . As we were going there, my sister died as was buried by a lone tree. We went on and never saw her grave again. She was eight years old.[3]

The family went as far as Council Bluffs, where they would stay for two years working to save enough money to continue the journey west toward safety. At this time, the family lived in a small log cabin with a sod chimney. The cloth-covered window kept out the harsh drafts. Sarah worked for fifty cents a week to earn money for supplies and clothing to continue west.[4] In June 1852, the family was ready. Sarah was seventeen years old as they began their journey. They belonged to a company of fifty wagons captained by Daniel Mark Burbank. She writes:

Daniel Mark Burbank was our Captain. Then we went on our way among the Indians. At night we had to guard the oxen so they would not steal them. . . . We dug a hole in the ground, put a skillet in the hole with a tight lid on it, put buffalo chips on the lid and set it on fire. It baked the bread fine. That is the way we did our cooking until . . . there was wood again.

Then we went along the Platte River where cholera broke out in the camp. Our Captain Daniel Mark Burbank's wife Abigail was one of the first to die. She was buried in a coffin along the river along with others that died with this disease. We had to go on in the morning and not ever to see their graves again. The night that Abigail died the wolves were howling. A young lady and I were the only ones to wash and dress her with what we could find. . . . We sewed her up in a sheet and quilt. That was all that could be done for her burial. The other women in the camp were afraid to prepare the bodies for burial . . . for fear of catching the cholera.[5]

The wagon train traveled on, covering between five and fifteen miles per day. About two months after Abigail died, Sarah became Daniel Burbank's wife, also taking on the role of nurse and mother to Abigail's four young children. She writes: "*I married Daniel . . . on the plains. Captain John B Walker . . . married us one evening. . . . We had cedar torch lights instead of candles. It was by the Green River in September. There I mothered four children that were sick with the scarlet fever. My husband and I had great trouble with sickness the rest of the way.*"[6]

One event caused great fear in Sarah during the crossing. When her husband was out hunting buffalo, a party of a hundred Indians took him captive. At first it appeared they would kill him, but the pioneers were able to ransom him for flour, sugar, and coffee from their dwindling supplies. Other scary experiences included jumping from a speeding wagon during a stampede to save a baby and crossing rivers swollen with spring floods.

The group reached the Salt Lake Valley in the fall of 1852. The growing family settled in Grantsville. Shortly thereafter, Sarah gave birth to the first of four children that would be born to the couple. Little George was welcomed by his older half-siblings, Mary, Daniel, Abigail, and Laura. Daniel Burbank had already felt the loss of two wives and two sons. The new child bound the family closer together. Another son, Brigham, and two daughters, Olive and Deseret, would join the family later, and nine others over the years, making thirteen in all.[7] Sarah began to serve at this time as the community midwife, working to help other neighbors bring new life safely into the harsh pioneer landscape. After ten years, in 1863, they were asked to settle Box Elder County, near present-day Brigham City. Both she and Daniel served actively in their church and community for the remainder of their lives. She and her husband were known for their gift of healing. She writes:

> *I remember my husband telling me that when, Emma, the Prophet's wife, was given up for dead by the doctor, he called Daniel . . . to come and see her. [Daniel] said, I can cure her. He went to the store and got medicine and stayed two nights and days and cured her. The Prophet told [my husband] to gather all his books together and to tend those in confinement. The knowledge that Daniel . . . had was received in a hospital. . . . The Prophet said that was his mission on earth, to attend the sick. His blessing also said that I came to this earth to attend the sick. . . . I have prayed for my parents who were very sick and they have recovered. When I have been in confinement cases, the Lord has blessed me in delivering women when they were in a very serious condition.*[8]

Sarah was later licensed by the Board of Medicine to practice obstetrics in Utah in 1893.

Daniel passed away age seventy-nine, but Sarah would go on to live another thirty-three years. She never remarried, stating that she *"had one good husband and she would not find another like him."*[9] Sarah passed on at the age of ninety-two, active to the end, and was buried beside her husband in Brigham City, Utah.[10]

NOTES

1. *Journal of Sarah Southworth Burbank*, LDS Church Historical Archives, accepted 1950. 34.

2. Margaret H. Halliday, "Sarah Southworth Burbank," www.rawlins .org, 1–2.

3. *Journal of Sarah Southworth Burbank*, 33.
4. Ibid., 33.
5. Ibid.
6. Ibid, 33–34.
7. Ibid., 36
8. Ibid, 34.
9. "Sarah Southworth Burbank," 1–2.
10. *Journal of Sarah Southworth Burbank*, 36.

ANNIE BRYCEON LAKER

July 12, 1832–August 19, 1921

*"My one desire is that I shall never do anything
to cause another pain."*[1]

ANNIE WAS THE SEVENTH OF ELEVEN CHIL-dren born to William Bryceon and Mary Tickell in Middlesex,[2] England, on July 12, 1832. Her parents were hard working and provided a happy home life for the frail Annie, who could not attend school till her later years due to her frequent illnesses.[3] Her family mostly belonged to the Methodist church, with her father acting as a city missionary and her two brothers as ministers. Annie enjoyed going to church and study-ing the Bible. One day she came across missionaries of the Mormon faith preaching in the streets that infant baptism was wrong. Annie was intrigued and stopped to listen. This information answered a longing in her heart, for her two youngest brothers had perished without baptism in an outbreak of the black measles.[4] Annie began to secretly attend the missionary meetings while maintaining her attendance at the Methodist church. One day, an elder from her family's church was visiting "to offer condolences over the loss of the two boys. He said, 'It is too bad that the boys were not baptized. Now they cannot be saved.' Annie, who was present, said, *'Oh, that is not so. Little children cannot sin and have no need of baptism. They go right into the presence of their Heavenly Father.'"*[5] Her father was outraged and forbade her to continue her studies with the Mormons. After joining The Church of Jesus Christ of Latter-day Saints, her family "ostracized her from her

home"[6] and she found gainful employment working with the family physician as he attended the sick and women in confinement.[7] She learned much that would strengthen in times to come. Little did she know that someday she would be the only person with medical training for over one hundred miles. In 1851, Annie was introduced to a silversmith known as Lashbrook Laker. They courted and soon married. He initially sought to refute Annie's faith through study of the scripture but instead was convinced of the truth of the gospel and baptized in 1853.[8] They were married on August 19, 1855 and that September departed for America aboard the ship *Emerald Isle*. They lived in New York, where Lashbrook worked as a silversmith[9] and Annie as a seamstress. They adopted a small boy, whose mother was a drunkard, and named him William Thomas Laker. He passed away at the age of four.[10] The young family moved to Wallingford, Connecticut, where their first baby was born, a girl they named Eva Anna, who lived only three weeks. In the next two years two more daughters would arrive, Amy and Sarah.

In 1861, the Laker family joined the Doolittle Company[11] and crossed the plains to Utah. They initially lived in Grantsville, where Annie began to put her medical skills to use. They had some trouble with the native population until Annie helped heal one of their children from a sickness.[12] She was never afraid of the Indians and would always help them if asked. In 1864, they were called to settle the Bear Lake Valley in Idaho. As winter set in, they had to live in their wagon box while Lashbrook worked to finish a cabin in time. Annie bore a daughter, Elizabeth, during a violent rainstorm at this time, while pots were placed on her bed to catch the freezing water.[13] The decision was soon made to send three of the men to Logan to obtain flour. They were delayed by blizzards and took three weeks to return home. Annie and the little girls lived on a pint of flour per day, praying for their safe return. Lashbrook built the first home in St. Charles, and the family lived in this location for many years. Soon another daughter, Elnora, and finally a son, Lashbrook,[14] joined the family. The couple took in over ten foster children as well during their time here.[15] Annie was the "main obstetrical woman"[16] in the settlement and served in this capacity for over twenty-six years. She would go anytime and in any condition of the weather, even if her own health was poor. In addition to her medical services, Annie also worked hard in her calling as the Bear Lake Stake Primary President, an office that she held into her eighties. A grandson, Alonzo, relates, "To know her was to love her. I find that every grown man or woman who as boys and girls in her primary organization, delights in claiming membership in her

primary."[17] Annie herself writes *"In 1880 [I] was chosen as Stake Primary President which position I still hold this 2nd day of December 1910. The Lord has blessed [me] and strengthened me in my work, and I rejoice to know that I have ever striven to perform my work faithfully and well."*[18] Annie was known for her generosity, her constant devotion to the gospel, and her willingness to serve all who called on her. As a midwife, when she saw babes alone and bereft of their mothers, she would take them into her own home and raise them until their families could provide for them. In the wintertime, she would often ride "to her cases in a bobsled, though she sometimes rode on horseback, sitting behind the man who had come for her."[19] She never used instruments even in difficult cases, but worked only with her hands. She developed an herbal formula useful in stopping hemorrhages as well as many other medicines.[20] She could set broken bones, treat burns, and would wash and lay out the deceased. Annie was greatly admired. She passed away at the age of eighty-nine and was buried by the side of her husband who had preceded her in death. Her funeral was widely attended. She asked that the following thought be carved on her headstone: *"My one desire is that I shall never do anything to cause another pain."*[21]

NOTES

1.   Catherine Wright Campbell, *Biography of Annie Bryceon Laker*, archived by International Society of Daughters of Utah Pioneers, May 21, 1997, 4.

2.   Ibid.

3.   Annie Bryceon Laker, "Memories," submitted by grandson Alonzo Laker Cook, archived by International Daughters of Utah Pioneers, February 26, 1934.

4.   Ibid., 2.

5.   Ibid.

6.   *Biography of Annie Bryceon Laker*, 1.

7.   "Memories," 3

8.   Ibid., 4.

9.   Claire Noall, "Mormon Midwives," *Utah Historical Quarterly* 10 (1942), 121.

10.   "Memories," 4.

11.   Ibid., 5.

12.   *Biography of Annie Bryceon Laker*, 2.

13.   "Mormon Midwives," 121.

14.   "Memories," 6.

15.   *Biography of Annie Bryceon Laker*, 3.

16. "Mormon Midwives," 121.
17. "Memories," 1.
18. Ibid.
19. "Mormon Midwives," 122.
20. Ibid.
21. *Biography of Annie Bryceon Laker,* 4.

EMMA LOUISE
BATCHELOR LEE FRENCH

April 21, 1836–November 16, 1897

English convert and pioneer who courageously settled the barren
wilderness of Southern Utah, loyal wife and widow, nurse and
midwife to settler and native alike.

MMA LOUISE BATCHELOR WAS BORN ON
April 21, 1836, in Uckfield, Sussex, England. She was converted
to the Church by missionaries along with her good friend Elizabeth Summers and soon desired to emigrate to Utah. She knew the hardships of the footsore handcart pioneers in the famous Willie and Martin
Handcart Companies. Having embarked across the plains too late in the
season of 1856, these two groups suffered extreme cold and starvation, losing
nearly two hundred people before being rescued by wagons sent through
the snow by Brigham Young.[1] Emma was left with others at Fort Laramie,
and she became a nursemaid to the family of Paul Gourley, whose wife was
expecting and ill. Emma delivered Mrs. Gourley's baby on the plains, her
first such experience. Her granddaughter writes: "Grandmother put the
baby and Mrs. Gourley into her handcart and pulled them on into the Great
Salt Lake Valley. It was during this . . . time that Mr. Gourley became sick
with the fever and so she put him into the cart also, and he finished the
trip in this manner. Mrs. Gourley always said that Emma was an angel of
the Lord, and their life preserver."[2] When Emma arrived in the valley, she
met and married John Kippen, who by all accounts, treated her unkindly.

Brigham Young, upon hearing of her plight from the bishop, released her from her marriage and invited her to stay a while at the Beehive House. On January 7, 1858, she was sealed by Brigham Young to John Doyle Lee, an adopted son of Young and prominent colonist.[3] Unknown to Emma, John had been involved in the terrible Mountain Meadows Massacre incident, in which 120 members of the Arkansas Fancher immigrant party were slain by Indians and Mormon settlers in a tragic misunderstanding.[4] The couple set up house on a dairy farm in Fort Harmony, Utah. This would be the most prosperous and peaceful period of Emma's life, and several children were born to John and Emma. As pressure to prosecute John for his involvement in the Mountain Meadows Massacre grew, John was asked by Young "to establish a ferry crossing on the Colorado River . . . [at] the only place between Moab, Utah, and Needles, California, where a wagon could easily be driven to the river's banks from either side. Fathers Dominguez and Escalante attempted to cross at the spot [in 1776], which they called *Salsipuedes* ('get out if you can!')"[5] John and several of his wives, including Emma, arrived at the site of the crossing where the ferry was to be built in 1871. Upon seeing her new home, a barren, hot, harsh red-clay terrain with soaring cliffs all around, Emma exclaimed, "*Oh, what a lonely dell.*"[6] Several days later Emma birthed a baby girl in her wagon as there was no other shelter and named her Lonely Dell.[7] The family set to work and soon had an operating ferry, housing, corrals, orchards, and crops. The Paria River was dammed with scrub brush and rocks to provide irrigation water, and the dam frequently washed out during flash floods and had to be replaced while the women and children carried buckets to water the plants by hand.[8] In the summer of 1873, John went into hiding. Emma kept the ferry in operation all this time. In 1874, Emma felt hard labor pains strike when John was away. Assisted by her fifteen-year-old son, Emma gave birth to a daughter named Victoria Elizabeth for her former queen.[9] Emma's bravery can also be seen in the following account:

> One day, while John was gone and she was alone with the children, she and William [her son] ferried a band of Navajos across the river. They were on their way to trade blankets for horses. They had to stay all night at the ferry. They stood around the small trading post talking and said, "We don't need to go any further for horses and cattle, we will burn the house and the family and take the stock here." They did not know that Emma understood their language. She said nothing, but she was worried. She prayed silently for wisdom as to what she should do. They did the chores as usual, and then she took her bedding for herself and her

children and spread it down in the Indian camp. She also took food, pots and pans and ate supper with the Navajos.

The Chief asked why she had come to sleep with them in their camp. She said, "*I don't think you will steal from me while I am watching you.*" She put the small children to bed, and after a while, she and the older boys retired. She pretended to be sound asleep, as though she had no fear of them. When the night was far spent and the stars in the right place, one of the Navajos said, "Now is the time for the killing." "No," said the Chief, "She brave woman."[10]

John Lee next spent the next three years in jail and participating in two separate trials. Emma remained supportive of him during this difficult time and would bring him food. On March 23, 1877, John was executed by firing squad.[11]

In 1879, the Church purchased the ferry from Emma for a fair sum, and Emma took her eight children to the White Mountains to start a ranch. Shortly thereafter, "the Indians went on the war path" and burnt the farm and stole the livestock. Emma started over again in Holbrook, Arizona, with a small farm and boarding house. Later, she moved to "Hardy Station," a small outpost close to Winslow, Arizona. Emma continued her constant care to cowboy, rancher's wife, native, or ruffian. She gave her midwifery and nursing services away to any who called whether they could pay or not. She would also collect used clothing to provide to the destitute pioneers crossing through, remembering her own experience crossing the plains.[12] In 1892, she married Frank French and continued her medical practice from the small farm they built on the Little Colorado. Emma suffered a fatal stroke at age sixty-one on November 16, 1897. As news that she was dying spread across the territory, people came "from far and near to offer assistance."[13] The minister who preached her liturgy praised her as a Good Samaritan. Emma was throughout her life a Lord's angel.[14]

NOTES

1. Jeffrey D. Nichols, "Courageous Emma Lee Endured Many Hardships in Pioneer Utah," *History Blazer* (July 1995).

2. Lucille M. Bevan, "History of Emma Batchelor," submitted to Daughters of Utah Pioneers, archived 1945.

3. "History of Emma Batchelor"; "Courageous Emma Lee Endured Many Hardships in Pioneer Utah."

4. Ibid.

5. "Courageous Emma Lee Endured Many Hardships in Pioneer Utah."

6. "History of Emma Batchelor."

7. Ibid.

8. Clarissa B. Workman, "History of Emma Batchelor," submitted by Lucille M. Bevan to International Society of Daughters of Utah Pioneers, no date, 1.

9. Ibid., 2.

10. Ibid., 1.

11. "Courageous Emma Lee Endured Many Hardships in Pioneer Utah," 2.

12. "History of Emma Batchelor," 2–3

13. Ibid., 3.

14. "Courageous Emma Lee Endured Many Hardships in Pioneer Utah," 2; Workman, 3.

ANN BROOKS ANDRUS

December 7, 1832–January 25, 1913

*Pioneer, mother, teacher, talented pianist, convert from England,
and midwife of Holladay*

A
NN BROOKS WAS BORN ON DECEMBER 7, 1832, in London, England, to James Simpkins and Elizabeth Brooks. Ann's father died early in life, and both Ann and her mother were receptive to the missionaries who proselyted in London and preached the doctrine of eternal families.[1] Ann and Elizabeth both immigrated to the United States and joined the Saints in Missouri. Ann, an accomplished musician, earned a living by teaching school and music lessons, eventually saving enough for passage to Utah in a wagon train. Ann also purchased a "lovely square grand piano,"[2] which she intended to bring to Utah. Either prior to their departure or after their arrival in Utah (the records are conflicting), Ann and her mother would become plural wives of Captain Milos Andrus, a strong man who led the wagon train to Utah.[3] Ann's piano and its weight posed a hardship to the wagon train, so after several weeks of travel, the decision was made to leave the piano on the east side of the

Missouri River, and continue on. "The piano was lifted off the wagon and left. It was then that Milo learned that Ann was missing. . . . he was told that she had stayed with her piano on the Iowa side of the Missouri River. [Milo] returned and then crossed the river . . . and brought Ann and her piano back to the company," and they carried it the rest of the eight hundred miles to Salt Lake City.[4] It was the second and only other piano to be brought to Utah, and it remained a source of delight for years to come.[5] Ann taught countless lessons to all who were willing to learn.[6]

According to descendants, Ann was "dignified, friendly and had a winning personality. . . . She was a well educated woman, becoming a school teacher."[7] Her most valuable contribution to her community, however, was her medical knowledge and willingness to nurse the sick. Ann served as the local midwife of Holladay and Cottonwood and was also on duty for every other kind of health concern. She brought a cheerful presence to the sickroom. Her granddaughter, Alice B. Casto, relates: "She knew much about medicine and the treatment of any deformity. She kept many remedies in her home and followed what she understood to be 'the rules of good health' that helped one remain well."[8] Ann ingeniously developed her own set of splints to correct a case of bilateral clubfoot that one of her grandchildren was born with. Ann was able to empathize with her patients when they grieved over the death of a loved one, having lost two of her five children when they were young.[9]

Ann had many interests and remained active in her roles until three weeks before her death. Her granddaughter relates: "I think the reason Grandmother stayed young in spirit until her death at 81 years was because she kept up with the interests of the day. She knew the name of the most popular song and the style of the latest dress, and enjoyed going to the theatre."[10] "Another experience I had with her was the dedication of the Salt Lake Temple . . . on April 6, 1893. As I was very young at the time, the thing that impressed me the most was the beautiful singing of the Hosanna Anthem . . . and the huge crowd all joining in the Hosanna shout."[11]

Ann passed away peacefully at the home of her daughter in Holladay, Utah, on January 25, 1913. Her attitude was so cheerful and her spirit so strong, that few knew of her daily struggles with severe arthritis. In the early morning, it would take her nearly an hour to massage her limbs enough that she could walk down the stairs, but she refused to let anyone wait on her or make a bed for her below. She remained available to help those in need to her last moments. Both she and her mother are buried in the Holladay Cemetery.[12]

NOTES

1.   Alice B. Casto, *Memories of Grandma (Ann Brooks Andrus)*, submitted to International Society of Daughters of Utah Pioneers, 1944. 1.

2.   International Society of Daughter of Utah Pioneers, *Pioneer Women of Faith and Fortitude*, various authors, compiled and submitted, 1998.

3.   *Memories of Grandma (Ann Brooks Andrus)*, 1.

4.   Ibid., 2.

5.   Ibid.

6.   Ibid.

7.   Ibid.

8.   Ibid., 3.

9.   Ibid., 4.

10. Ibid., 1.

11. Ibid., 3.

12. Ibid., 4.

PAULINA ELIZA PHELPS LYMAN

March 20, 1827–October 11, 1912

Pioneer, adoptive mother, seamstress extraordinaire, widow, midwife and surgeon, farmer

BORN TO MORRIS CHARLES PHELPS AND LAURA Clark on March 20, 1827, in Lawrence, Illinois, Pauline gained the benefit of early teaching at the knees of her parents. Early converts to the Church and staunchly loyal during the harsh persecutions of that time, Paulina's parents seeded a kernel of faith in her heart that would sustain her through the many dif-
ficult trials she would face. Paulina was blessed by her father shortly after her birth while he was incarcerated on false charges along with Parley P. Pratt and others. Her strong mother was able to smuggle out the manuscript "Key to The-ology," from the prison by sewing it into her underskirts. When five years of age, Paulina was blessed by Joseph Smith that she would come to the Rocky Mountains, a prophecy far beyond the imagination of those gathered to hear. Paulina had a melancholy childhood punctuated by the

early death of her mother when Paulina was fourteen. She quickly assumed care of the remaining eight children and hired out to other families to keep food on the table.[1]

Five years later, we find her joined in plural marriage to apostle Amasa Mason Lyman on January 16, 1846, in the Nauvoo Temple. We see her courage as she drives a four-horse team across the plains to Winter Quarters for Sidney Tanner, nursing his sick wife along the way, and pregnant herself. When Mr. Tanner's wife succumbed to illness, she took care of their eight children as well. A few months later, she would bear her first child in the cold privation of that temporary refuge of the Saints.[2]

After waiting for a year, Paulina arrived with her baby in the Salt Lake Valley in October 1848. The family wintered in the fort. Food was so scarce, and a pound of flour sold for $1.00.[3] Amasa had brought a bale of cotton home when he returned from his mission to the Southern states. Paulina carefully spun and wove the raw cotton into carpets, jeans, tablecloths, and bedspreads, which she sold, using the money to buy food. She only had enough to allow her baby a spoonful of flour per day. [4]

Amasa was soon sent with some of his family to colonize California. In the meantime, Paulina went with her children to settle in Parowan. She lived with Brother Jess Smith until a house could be built.[5] Some time later, "her sister wife," Cornelia L. Lyman, with her boys came to live with her. She cared for Cornelia until she passed on, and then raised her young boys as her own. Paulina was known well for her industriousness and kindness. Her services as a seamstress were sought after,[6] despite living in a time when nearly all women were skilled at sewing. She was always helping others and exemplified the heart of charity. Perhaps this attitude motivated her to travel to Salt Lake and take a course in obstetrics under Dr. Ellis R. Shipp. With her large family, this would have been a remarkable feat for anyone to undertake, let alone a sixty-year-old widow. Having lost two of her own seven children at a tender age, Paulina was probably especially motivated to learn how to save lives.

She returned to Parowan and established a successful medical practice, delivering over five hundred babies, performing minor surgeries, setting bones, and tending the sick.[7] She pioneered vaccination against smallpox disease in southern Utah.[8] Her time belonged to those in need. The tall and slight midwife related, *"Why, I've driven my horse belly-deep in the mud with the wheels of the buggy sunk to the hub to get to some of my patients."*[9] We learn more about her from her son William H. Lyman:

What I am able to give will be from my recollection of my mother's work. Of course it is remarkable and rather unusual for a woman of her age to enter school and take training as she did. In the time that she had outside of her professional work as a midwife, she practiced medicine in a general way, and was busy most of the time, taking care of the sick with various ailments. I will attempt to relate a few of the outstanding cases that she treated. One remarkable incident was the case of a young girl who, in playing with a powder can, ignited it. The explosion burned her face until all the skin on it hung in blisters and rags. Mother applied linseed oil all over her face and them put a mask on, covering her entire face and then varnished it with varnish. Her face healed up under the treatment. When the mask was taken off there was not a scar to be seen. She had many patients afflicted with typhoid fever, and scarlet fever and was extremely successful in her practice. . . .

The small fee that she received for her services caused her to depend on those she served. I remember one incident where the Indians were camped about eight miles west of Parowan, near the town of Summit. A young Indian squaw was confined. The women about her became alarmed, and a squaw was sent a distance of about two miles to the town of Summit in order to get help. A man in Summit hooked his team up on a lumber wagon and drove through the mud to Parowan to get mother's assistance. During the time she was getting her satchel and preparing to make the trip, the old squaw who had accompanied the man from Summit, made a hurried tour of the neighbors to collect some food to take back to the camp. When they arrived, the children of the camp gathered around the old squaw and she divided the food out to them. Mother waited on the young squaw and saved the baby, and arrived home safely after having a rather rough ride. After witnessing the hunger of the children in the camp, she resolved never to turn Indians away from her door without giving them some food.

Her services were required in the neighboring towns of Paragonah and Summit. The father of the family usually came with a wagon or sleigh. When she finished her training under Mrs. Shipp, she was set apart by an apostle [Franklin D. Richards]. She was promised in that blessing that she should know on the impulse of the moment what to do when she entered the sickroom.[10]

Paulina was known for her inspired aid in times of trouble. She worked as a midwife "almost until her death, which came October 11, 1912."[11]

NOTES

1. Kate B. Carter, "Pauline Eliza Phelps Lyman," in *Heart Throbs of the West*, vol. 3 (Salt Lake City: Daughters of Utah Pioneers, 1951), summarized in Lyman Archives, www.lymanites.org/lyman/archives/pioneerhistory/paulineelizaphelpslyman.asp.

2. Elizabeth S. Wilcox, "Interview." Published in *Utah Historical Quarterly* 10 (1942), 118.

3. Eugene Campbell, "A History of the Church of Jesus Christ of Latter-day Saints in California," PhD diss., University of Southern California, 1952.

4. "Pauline Eliza Phelps Lyman."

5. Ibid.

6. Ibid.

7. "Interview," 119.

8. "Pauline Eliza Phelps Lyman."

9. "Interview," 119.

10. William H. Lyman, "Letter," published in *Utah Historical Quarterly*, 10 February 1942, 119–120.

11. Ibid.

ROMANIA BUNNELL
PRATT PENROSE

August 8, 1839–November 9, 1932

Physician, mother, feminist, pioneer, missionary, and innovator

IN WASHINGTON, INDIANA, ON AUGUST 8, 1839 A baby girl was born to Luther Bunnell and Ester Mendenhall. Her parents were members of the Church[1] and made the journey to Nauvoo when Romania was seven to be closer to the main body of Saints. Hardship and persecution awaited the family there. Education was very important to her father,[2] and he sacrificed to make sure that Romania was able to attend several schools, includ-ing "the Western Agricultural School, the Quaker Institute of Ohio, and the Female Seminary at Crawfordsville, Indiana."[3] Desiring to join the exodus to Utah, but lacking the means to do so, Romania's father left to join the gold rush in California. Ironically, after making enough to send for his family, he died, and the family was never able to receive his earnings.[4] Mrs. Bunnell returned to her husband's house and saved enough together for the journey west. Joining an independent company of wagons in 1855

led by Captain John Hendley, they made the trek across the plains. Her mother tenderly carted her prize piano all of the two thousand miles. They could not have arrived at a more difficult time. The Saints were starving due to crop failure, and flour was twenty-five dollars a barrel (a month's wages, equivalent to $2,500 today.)

At the age of twenty, Romania married Parley P. Pratt Jr. on February 23, 1859. They were soon blessed with several children. Tragically, two of her young children died before the age of three. This would affect Romania deeply and kindle within her a strong desire to ensure that any person in need would have access to medical care.[5] With a nursing infant in her arms, Brigham Young asked her to go back east to study medicine, stating that "Women must come forth as doctors in these valleys of the mountains."[6] Brigham felt it was extremely improper for a male physician to attend to the care of women. Lacking the necessary money, Romania sold the piano that her mother had so carefully hauled across the plains. With a heart-wrenching good-bye to her family of five, she set off for New York City, leaving her children in the care of her mother.[7] After studying for a year, she returned home, broke but inspired. Finally she was understanding the mysteries of the body and learning how to ease its suffering. Assisted by Brigham Young, she went back to complete her training at the Women's Medical College of Pennsylvania, graduating in 1877 with her friend Dr. Ellis R. Shipp. She was the first native daughter to become a doctor. Returning to Utah, she began practicing general medicine and obstetrics. "After two years of general practice, feeling the need of further training, she went to New York City, where she took courses in diseases of the eye and ear."[8] After her training, she was able to perform the first cataract operation in Utah. Asked by Zina Young to teach her skills to others,[9] she established the Relief Society Nurses department.[10]

She divorced Parley four years after returning home, the couple unable to reconcile Romania's strong passion for medicine and women's suffrage. Indeed, Romania was a woman who spoke her mind and gave advice in a tone that most patients dare not disobey.[11] Her interests were broad and she served with enthusiasm in many diverse areas of the Church such as president of the Retrenchment Society (forerunner of the Young Women organization). Romania served on the board of Deseret Hospital,[12] along with contemporaries Drs. Ellis R. Shipp, Zina Young, Emmeline Wells, and Phoebe Woodruff.[13] Indeed, these women along with Dr. Ellen Ferguson first developed the idea of a Mormon community hospital and implemented their plans to provide care to all.

In her later years, she married Apostle Charles W. Penrose and was a good companion to him during his call to serve as mission president in Britain and Europe.[14] Penrose was a professor of theology at Brigham Young University, an editor of the *Deseret News*, and in well known for his hymns and missionary tracts. Romania was a good match for him in her ardency for her faith and woman's rights. While accompanying him during his mission, she served as the Utah delegate to the International Woman Suffrage Alliance Conference in Amsterdam. She also organized the first Relief Societies in Europe.[15]

Despite her expertise in curing illnesses of the eye, Romania spent her last days in darkness, blind for unknown reasons. She died at the age of ninety-three, surrounded by her posterity.

NOTES

1.   Marie Mackey, "Up the Rugged Hill of Knowledge: Romania Pratt Penrose," in *Heroines of the Restoration*, Salt Lake City, Bookcraft, 1997.

2.   Ibid.

3.   Blanche E. Penrose, "Early Utah Medical Practice: Women Doctors" *Utah Historical Quarterly* 10 (1942): 28.

4.   Ibid.

5.   "Up the Rugged Hill of Knowledge: Romania Pratt Penrose."

6.   Ibid.

7.   "Early Utah Medical Practice: Women Doctors," 28.

8.   Ibid., 29.

9.   Ibid.

10.   "Up the Rugged Hill of Knowledge: Romania Pratt Penrose,"

11.   "Early Utah Medical Practice: Women Doctors," 29

12.   Ibid.

13.   Andrew Jenson, *Latter-day Saint Biographical Encyclopedia*, vol. 4. (Salt Lake City, UT: *Deseret News*, 1943), 193.

14.   "Early Utah Medical Practice: Women Doctors," 29

15.   "Up the Rugged Hill of Knowledge: Romania Pratt Penrose."

GEORGIA LATHOURIS
MAGERAS "MAGEROU"

1868–1950

"Scream, push! You've got a baby in there, not a pea in a pod!"[1]

AMONG THE EARLY SETTLERS OF UTAH AND surrounding territories were Greek immigrant families drawn to the area and the promise of a better life. They added color and flavor to the melting pot of nationalities joining the Mormon settlements out West. One particularly memorable woman was the Greek midwife "Magerou."

Georgia was born in a remote village of Greece in the late 1860s. Little is known regarding her early history other than that she frequently took food to her brothers and father as they watched their flocks grazing in the hills. On one such occasion, a woman called to her asking for assistance as she labored in the open fields, unable to reach home. With the simple direction of the mother, Georgia was able to safely deliver the baby, beginning a long and successful career in medicine. She was only fourteen at the time. A few years later, she married Nikos Mageras, who saw her value despite her lack of dowry. Their native country was in the throes of war and revolution. The young couple fled to America hoping to find a land to support their dreams. In 1909, the family arrived in Utah, settling in Snaketown (west of Magna.)

"Magerou," as she came to be known, was soon very busy assisting at the births in her local community. Many of the men wanted a girl from

home and paid to acquire picture brides from Greece. According to historian Helen Z. Papanikolas, "not only Greek but Italian, Austrian and Slavic women called Magerou at all hours. They preferred her to the company doctors."[2] It is noteworthy that in all her time attending to women, she never lost a mother or an infant. This has been attributed to her fastidious cleanliness. At a birth, water was boiling, sheets and blankets were warming, her hands were vigorously scrubbed, and often she would copy the new medical practice of donning rubber gloves. "Magerou took care of her patients with the efficiency of a contemporary obstetrician. While olive oil and baby blankets were kept warm in coal stove ovens, she boiled cloths, kept water hot, cut her fingernails, scrubbed her arms and hands well, and after observing American doctors using alcohol and rubber gloves, she added these to her accoutrements . . . small though she was, her voice carried through the neighborhoods exhorting, shouting, *Scream, push! You've got a baby in there, not a pea in a pod!"*[3]

Magerou would then see that the mother was washed and well fed, would braid her hair, and often would help with the house chores for several days.

Georgia also met the health care needs of others in the area. The immigrants were not used to American ways and clung to their native beliefs in "the evil eye," and other such traditions. Though we are not sure if Magerou believed in these traditions, she did not laugh at them and would practice folk remedies, burning holy incense and sprinkling holy water as necessary, thus caring for the psychospiritual needs of her community as well. She would often recite the Lord's Prayer during her treatments, invoking God's help in her endeavors. Georgia was not only found at the bedside of laboring women. She was also skilled in helping patients with pneumonia, relieving backaches, and setting bones. She developed a cast made of resin, egg whites, and wool. Hot mustard plasters and whiskey with cloves were used in cases of lung disease. On at least two occasions, her quick actions saved the legs of severely injured men, which the local doctor had determined to perform amputations on.

During the years, the Mageras family were residents of Murray, Tooele, and Magna. Patients would travel great distances to see her, though they had medical assistance closer to home. Through it all, Magerou also experienced the loss of some of her own children, racial discrimination, venomous editorials against the Greeks in the newspaper, and attacks by the Ku Klux Klan. Through it all she ardently maintained the attitude that time would bring a solution. Papanikolas writes, "The many pictures of her show

a smiling serene woman appearing much younger than she was. . . She was stoic over the deaths of her own infants and family reverses. She endured without knowing that she did. The feast days of her church gave her life order and happiness."[4] The Greek midwife Magerou remains an icon of the indomitable spirit of the pioneer woman.

NOTES

1.   Helen Z. Papanikolas, "Magerou: The Greek Midwife," *Utah Historical Quarterly* 38 (Winter 1970): 50–60

2.   Murphy, Miriam B. "The Greek Midwife Magerou," *History Blazer* (February 1996), 1.

3.   Ibid., 2.

4.   Ibid.

HILDA ANDERSON ERICKSON

November 11, 1859–January 1, 1968

Midwife and doctor in Tooele Valley, missionary and friend of the Indians, pioneer mother, seamstress, farmer, car enthusiast

I N THE MOUNTAINS OF SWEDEN, A DAUGHTER
was born to Pehr Anderson and Marie Katrina Larsen on November 11, 1859. They named her Hilda, and she grew up with her four brothers learning the care of a home and how to farm. Her mother taught her sewing and lacework skills, which would prove invaluable in later years. Missionaries found the family in 1866, and soon Hilda along with her mother and younger brothers were bound for America, a trip that would take six months. Pehr and the two older boys remained at home to earn more money for passage. They traveled from Sweden to Denmark, then to Germany and England. After a nine-week sail aboard the *Cavour*, the family disembarked in New York in July. From there they took a train to St. Joseph, Missouri. The ferry from Missouri to Nebraska was complicated by an outbreak of cholera, which the

Anderson's were fortunate to survive. "*As soon as anyone of the cholera-smitten passengers died the captain steered for the nearest shore. There the men dug a grave and buried the corpse. Then the trip continued until it was time to steer to shore for the next funeral.*"[1] From there, they joined the last wagon train of the season to reach Salt Lake City. Hilda writes about this experience in her journal:. "*The trip from Wyoming, Nebraska, to Salt Lake City took an even ten weeks. We reached our destination on October 22, 1866. In Salt Lake City, they had been fearing that we would be snowbound, so they had sent out people with many mules to meet us. The mules pulled our wagons the last two days instead of our oxen, who were absolutely exhausted.*"[2]

The family settled in Mount Pleasant, staying with another family who had befriended them on the long trek. Marie took in sewing to pay the bills and sent the children to school with the little money she had left over. Hilda was seven at the time. Pehr and the older brothers were soon reunited with everyone and the family relocated to Grantsville. Hilda was able to stay in school until she was fourteen. She also took additional schooling in dress-making, tailoring, and patternmaking. At the young age of fifteen, Hilda began to support herself with her sewing. She was so industrious that she could turn out an entire dress, suit, or coat each day (by hand).[3] Her journal at the age of twenty-one reveals a confident, hard-working young woman who loved to dance and go to the theatre. She was wary of settling down, and it took the ardent pursuit of another Swedish immigrant John Erickson to convince her to marry. He was rebuffed in his pursuits numerous times, but the couple was finally joined in marriage on February 23, 1882. Hilda writes that after their marriage, "*We went downtown to buy again then down for supper and I was trying to get Lucy to stay with me but she would not. Alfred coaxed her to go with him then. JE [John Erickson, her new husband] stayed with me and I had a good bawl when they went.*"[4] Whatever trepidation may have accompanied Hilda on her wedding day, it was soon swallowed up in strong devotion and a life of service. Just one year after marriage, the couple was called to act as missionaries to the Goshute Indians in the Deep Creek Mountain Range in the Utah-Nevada border.[5] The land was extremely harsh and could only be reached by crossing the salt flat desert, where wagons and horses often became mired and frequent sand and windstorms blew. One of the unique items Hilda always carried in her medical bag was a buckskin mask with tiny slits for eyes and nose so that the desert conditions wouldn't peel off her skin as she rode to those who needed help.[6] The Church wanted to establish a large mission in this area, helping the natives learn to culti-vate, teaching them English and acquainting them with Mormon beliefs.

John and Hilda, together with two other couples were called to this difficult task. Hilda taught the women to read, write, spin, weave, and sew. She also taught them to bead, a skill the Goshutes are now famous for. After four years, the couple was blessed with a daughter, Amy. [7]

When Amy was still a toddler, Hilda left her in the care of her mother in Grantsville and went to Salt Lake to study obstetrical courses at Deseret Hospital taught by Dr. Romania P. Pratt. Hilda had seen the desperate need for medical care in the desert and was determined to do something about it.[8] In 1885, Hilda was licensed to practice obstetrics and medicine in Utah. Hilda returned home and began a successful and busy medical practice that included delivery and care of mothers and infants, dentistry, setting bones, healing burns and snakebites, and caring for the sick and those who had suffered myriad accidents. Many of her patients were the miners who roamed the region and often stopped into the ranch to visit the dry goods store that Hilda and John had started. Being a believer in good nutrition, Hilda produced dairy products (cheeses and butter), which she sold to the miners and gave to the Indian children to supplement their sparse diet. Hilda also served as the local veterinarian, riding sidesaddle to reach destinations as far as twenty-five miles away. We learn from her delivery logs about harsh conditions, long journeys, the difficulty of maintaining tiny lives in that territory, and her habit of knitting beautiful lace as she waited out a fever or difficult labor. The natives called her "Angapomy," or redhead, and held her in the highest regard.[9] She is known to have delivered over two hundred babies.[10]

In 1890 a son was born to John and Hilda, and the couple was released from their mission. John had spotted a piece of property he liked and they started their own outfit on Trout Creek in 1893. Neighbors scoffed at their plans and stated that nothing could be grown in that area. The Ericksons named it "Last Chance Ranch" and later that year gave a squash from their garden that was too heavy to carry to one of these neighbors.[11] John was very innovative and soon had a system of reservoirs and irrigation that allowed them to expand into the dairy business as well. The couple also raised sheep, cattle, hay, and wheat. After four years, John was called on a mission to Sweden, where he remained till 1909.[12] At the conclusion of his service, Hilda and her son traveled back to Sweden to visit their homeland. This was the first vacation Hilda ever had. [13]

Hilda had many other talents besides medical care. Her vegetable gardens were very productive. She was known for her lace-bedecked dwelling. Lace was one easily made luxury that made the barren desert seem more

survivable. In 1922 she was nominated to serve in the state legislature, though she never sought public office.[14] Hilda and John purchased a combination lumberyard, service station, and general store in Grantsville in 1925. She continued to run the store until two years after John's death in 1943; she was eighty-five.[15] Always a thrill-seeker, she was a passenger aboard the first jet plane to land in Salt Lake City. She was heard to remark, *"To think that in my day I have seen man fly like the birds, me a girl who came to this land on a wagon."*[16] She had a later habit of racing fast cars (she owned eleven) until her driver's license was suspended for speeding at the age of ninety-five.[17] "She was still voting at the age of 102. At the age of 104 she still went to the beauty shop, did her own housework, and took a daily walk."[18] She commented in an interview, *"If it weren't for the strong arms and wrists I got from pulling teeth, I don't know how I'd get along."*[19] Her bravery in the face of pioneering, mission work, solo medical practice, desert farming, widowhood, and changing technology was remarkable. Her willingness to serve those on the fringe of civilization is worth emulation. Hilda lived to the age of 108, passing away on January 1, 1968.[20]

NOTES

1. Jude Daurelle, "Buckskin, Lace and Forceps: Hilda Anderson Erickson, Utah Pioneer," *Piecework* (Nov./Dec., 1993), 43.

2. Ibid.; Hilda Erickson, *Journal*, archived by International Society of Daughters of Utah Pioneers. 2,3.

3. "Buckskin, Lace and Forceps," 44.

4. Catherine Wright Campbell, *Biography of Annie Bryceon Laker*, submitted to International Society of Daughters of Utah Pioneers, May 21, 1997, 3–4.

5. "Buckskin, Lace and Forceps," 44.

6. Ibid., 50.

7. Ibid., 44.

8. *Deseret News*, November 12, 1965.

9. Ibid.

10. Inger Bukke, "Stories from Your Museum, March Lesson: Hilda Andersson Erickson," submitted to International Society Daughters of Utah Pioneers, n.d., 1.

11. Harold H. Jenson, "Utah's Last Pioneer," *Salt Lake Tribune* November 1, 1964, 2.

12. Ibid.

13. Ibid.; "Buckskin, Lace, and Forceps," 49.

14. "Buckskin, Lace and Forceps," 49.

15. Ibid.

16. "Utah's Last Pioneer," 2.

17. "Buckskin, Lace and Forceps,"49

18. "Stories from Your Museum, March Lesson: Hilda Andersson Erickson," 1.

19. Ibid., 5.

20. "Buckskin, Lace and Forceps," 49.

JULINA LAMBSON SMITH

June 18, 1849–January 10, 1936

"It was always a joy for me to place a tiny one for the first time in its mother's arms, for I felt again the thrills that I felt on looking into my own babies' faces."[1]

JULINA LAMBSON WAS BORN ON JUNE 18, 1849, TO Alfred Boaz and Melissa Jane Bigler, sturdy pioneers of 1847. Her father was an excellent craftsman who built the first mills in the area and owned the first plastered house in the territory.[2] Julina had a happy childhood, though it was com- plicated by the privation of the sudden exodus to Nephi when Johnson's Army threatened. In her teen years, she spent a great deal of time at the home of her uncle, George A. Smith, keeper of church records. It was here that she became enamored of Joseph F. Smith.[3] The couple was married May 5, 1866, before Joseph would be called as an apostle and later President of the Church (1901–1918). We learn from family records that Julina undertook the study of obstetrics in order to assist her sister wives in childbirth.[4] She studied under Drs. Ellis and Margaret Shipp,

and soon began delivering babies in her own family and those of neighbors nearby. She was very successful in her practice and never lost a mother.[5] Julina's diary tells her story most eloquently:

> *"I was born of goodly parents who helped pioneer the way to Utah in the year 1847. My father, Alfred B. Lambson, was an excellent mechanic and blacksmith and his services were of great value to the company as they crossed the plains and to the people after he reached the valley, as will be found in history.*
>
> *My mother, Melissa Jane Bigler Lambson, was the youngest sister of our late Relief Society President, Bathsheba W. Smith. I was born June 18, 1849, in the home of my parents, which was the first home plastered in Salt Lake City.*
>
> *I married Joseph F. Smith May 5, 1866, before he was ordained an Apostle. Our first baby, Mercy Josephine, was born in 1867.*
>
> *In 1868, with my full consent, Joseph married Sarah Ellen Richards, a daughter of President Willard Richards, who was one year younger than I. We started our married lives together—mere girls—and for forty-seven years were companions.*
>
> *In 1869, a daughter was born to Sarah, but our Heavenly Father saw fit to leave her with us only a few days. When my second baby was only eight months old, the Angel of Death again visited us, this time bearing away my firstborn, our little chatterbox, the delight of our home.*
>
> *When the mother of three children, I studied Obstetrics and Nursing under the best physicians in Utah, and the knowledge acquired stood me in good stead not only in our own family but in hundreds of cases where I have responded to calls from expectant mothers. And it was always a joy for me to place a tiny one for the first time in its mother's arms, for I felt again the thrills that I felt on looking in to my own babies' faces. On the first of January 1871, with the consent of both Sarah and myself, Joseph married my sister Edna. Our lives have been so closely interwoven I cannot separate my life from theirs. Sarah had eleven and Edna ten children, but I claim them all, for I have watched and helped to care for them since they drew their first breath, and my life would be empty without them.* [Julina and Joseph had eleven children: Mercy Josephine, Mary Sophronia, Donette, Joseph Fielding, David Asael, George Carlos, Julina Clarissa, Elia Wesley, Emily Jane, Rachel and Edith Elenor.]
>
> *As our family increased in size, additions were made to the two original rooms of our dwelling until in time the roof covered nineteen rooms which formed three apartments, and housed a family of twenty-one.*[6]

Julina's book of records details the births she attended and shows an interesting side to Julina's life. When it was time for her own deliveries,

Edna Lambson Smith

she attended herself with Joseph's help. She had said to her husband, *"If you will help me, I can take care of myself."*[7] Later her younger sister Edna Lambson (March 3, 1851–February 28, 1926) would also take up the profession of midwifery and though not as engaged in the business as Julina, would faithfully serve for many years. Her son Joseph, who later became president of the LDS church, relates that he would often have to hitch up the buggy in the middle of the night, and if she was not home by morning, would prepare breakfast for his siblings.[8] Edna attended Julina during her last births. When the polygamy raids began to occur, Julina and Joseph left Salt Lake City and served a mission in Hawaii (Sandwich Islands) for two years. Julina had two children while serving here and was a midwife to the native population, attending one birth eleven days after she delivered her own son.[9] The native population dearly loved tiny Julina.[10] The couple returned to Salt Lake City and were soon busy with their respective duties again.

Julina had many other responsibilities, including president of the Retrenchment Society, member of the Relief Society board, instigator of the Burial Clothes Department, captain and charter member of Daughters of Utah Pioneers, and temple worker. After breaking her hip in 1925, she was forced to retire from public life.[11] Julina lived to eighty-six years and was survived by seventy-two grandchildren.

NOTES

1.   Julina Lambson, *Journal*, submitted to International Society Daughters of Utah Pioneers, 2.

2.   Claire Noall, "Mormon Midwives," *Utah Historical Quarterly* 10 (1942), 139.

3.   Joseph F. Smith, Jr., and John J. Stewart, *The Life of Joseph Fielding Smith*. (Salt Lake City: The Church of Jesus Christ of Latter-day Saints, 1972), 52–53.

4.   "Mormon Midwives," 140.

5.   Ibid., 141.

6.   Julina Lambson, *Journal*, 3.

7. "Mormon Midwives," 140.

8. *The Life of Joseph Fielding Smith.* 52–3.

9. "Mormon Midwives," 140–41.

10. Ibid., 141.

11. Andrew Jenson, *Latter-day Saint Biographical Encyclopedia*, vol. 4. (Salt Lake City, UT: *Deseret News*, 1943).

JOSEPHINE CATHERINE CHATTERLY WOOD

September 10, 1853–February 10, 1909

"No woman that was born upon the earth shall
have a greater crown and blessing"[1]

O N SEPTEMBER 7, 1853, JOSEPH CHATTERLY
breathed his last breath on earth after suffering an accidental
gunshot wound to the abdomen. Three days later his wife Catherine would bear him a tiny daughter named Josephine (Jody) in the young
pioneer town of Cedar City, Utah. The twice-widowed mother lay sick
with grief, but managed to struggle on.
Little is known of how the young family
of six managed. Catherine had been a
prosperous woman by all accounts until
she lost a great deal in the failure of the
iron mines and the crop destruction of
1855. Indeed, Josephine's mother passed
away the next year, leaving five orphaned
children.[2] Her oldest half-sister Mary,
a newly married woman, took all of the
children into her home and raised them.
Jody grew up under the stern hand of
her brother-in-law, William Cameron,
and benefited from a good education.[3]

We see a spark of her personality early on. She loved to draw so much that she would endure the slap of a ruler when caught drawing on her slate board at school.[4] As she grew, she began to work outside the home to contribute to her support. Often she was paid in food and other goods, but if she was given money, she was allowed to keep it. After saving pennies for a long time, she was finally able to purchase a pair of "store shoes." Though three sizes too big, they were a source of great pride and joy to her. [5]

During her teen years, Jody found work in Salt Lake. It was here that she became acquainted with Samuel Wood, whom she married in the Endowment House on Christmas Day, 1871, at the age of eighteen.[6] They returned to Cedar City, where Sam developed a thriving carpentry trade. Though financially prosperous, Sam and Jody suffered through the deaths of their firstborn son and daughter (to pertussis and scarlet fever, respectively.)[7]

In the spring of 1879, Sam was among those called to settle the San Juan area. Knowing of the rumors of resettlement, Jody had deliberately stayed home. Her half-sister Margaret came running into the house exclaiming, "O Josephine, you are called but surely you won't go." Sam followed behind her and said, "We are among those called and we will go."[8] Preparations began for the difficult trek. Almost three years later, with two additional children, the small family joined a company of wagons departing to settle the southern frontier. Jody and Sam said good-bye to their comfortable home, family and friends, the graves of their children, indeed, everything they had known.[9] We glimpse a taste of their feelings from excerpts of Jody's journal:

> *"We have been called on a Mission to help settle Bluff in San Juan County, and to make peace with the Indians. . . . Four families from Cedar left October 17, 1882, with aching hearts, after saying goodby [sic] to our loved ones, and the homes we loved, not knowing when, if ever, we would see them again, and not knowing where we were going."*

> *October 19 – "The children were cross all night. It is very cold. We camp at Little Creek Canyon—the children and even the cattle want to go back, and I long to see you tonight, but every day is taking us farther away."*

> *October 24 – "We are anxious to get over Escalante Mountain today. This road is just a trail, rock, fallen trees, and stumps in our path. The women and children walk most of the way to the top, with mothers carrying babies; then it started to sprinkle, so we got into the wagons and didn't take one good long breath until we reached the bottom."*

October 30 – "I don't know what this place is called, but I call it Devil's Twist, and that's a Sunday name for it. I cannot imagine any worse roads any place on earth. There is no use for me to try and describe it. This is the most God-forsaken and wild country I have ever seen, read or heard about. We hardly get started when they have to double horses on the wagons, the sand is so deep in places and in other places nothing but rocks. . . . The wind is blowing so bad we cannot see far ahead for the sand, and if we open our mouths, they will be filled. . . . No water again tonight, although the children are crying for it and it is very cold."

November 2 – "Over rocks, no human being should ever try to go over, but we kept going until we reached the dreaded Colorado River."

November 13 – "We are happy to get to Bluff. Our horses were tired out, so are we, but we got here alive."[10]

Jody was twenty-nine years old when she arrived to settle Bluff, and Sam was thirty-nine. Their old neighbor in Cedar City, Jens Nielson, was called to be the bishop of the struggling community. Perceiving the needs of his growing population, Bishop Nielson asked her to serve as the local midwife. She protested, *"I am as green as a cucumber and I don't know how babies are born!"* She was given a blessing that if she asked for the Lord's help in a delivery, He would show her what to do.[11] Humble Jody then sent for every available printed material on medicine. She was so afraid of her first "case" that she asked the bishop to accompany her. Upon assisting the mother, she observed that the baby had the cord around her neck. Unsure of what to do, she heard a voice whisper quick directions. After, she relates: "I thought Bishop Nielson had spoken to me, but when I turned to look at him, he was not in the room. I knew that the Lord had blessed me, telling me plainly what to do."[12]

We know a great deal about Jody's medical practice from the writings of others. Mrs. Lloyd Hansen, a long-time resident relates:

She nursed others when she should have been in bed herself. She suffered from sick headaches, and occasionally remained in bed for several days. On one of these occasions a call came for her to wait upon a woman who suffered from a similar ailment. Aunt Jody's husband and her children objected but the man was insistent saying if Aunt Jody would just come and go to bed in the same room, his wife would get better. For her to refuse was unheard of . . . the gentlemen got his team . . . and took her to his home. Later in the day, being anxious about their mother, her

daughters went to see how she was. The patient was asleep and Aunt Jody was resting.

She was afraid of the Indians, but through . . . her own kindness and generosity, the Indians learned to love [her] . . . [She] ministered to their needs. She learned from them much valuable information in the use of herbs in sickness.

One time when the men were away, Old Posey, the Ute outlaw, was drunk and came charging into the house yelling and swinging his gun and ordered something to eat. She was afraid, but boldly walked up to him and took the gun away. *'What's the matter with you, Posey? she said, 'You know we are your friends and we don't like you when you act like this.'* He ate and went away without his gun, being told he could have it when he acted like a friend. He came back the next day . . . and said, "Me Sammy Wood's squaw's friend.'

She was the doctor of Bluff for twenty-five years. She often gave her services free. . . . Her regular charge was $2.50 for a confinement; this included care for the mother and babe. She did their washing and their cooking for ten days and served longer if necessary.

One night a call came form Monticello, a town fifty miles away. It was winter; the weather was bitterly cold and the snow deep. There was no way for her to make the trip except on horseback. It did not enter her head to refuse. She and her son, Joseph, dressed themselves warmly, and made the trip in two days. . . .

Often the food was scarce, and when stranger or friend came to her door, she shared what she had, saying: 'Bread and butter with a welcome is better than a banquet without one.' She loved to do the thing she was called to do. She loved her husband and family. She never complained. God gave her wisdom and power because she could translate pain into joy."[13]

Jody's life was not immune to sorrow. Five of her ten children died early. She struggled with persistent migraines.[14] After several decades in Bluff, the family was called to move to Monticello. After serving this community for a short time, "Jody became very ill . . . [with what] is suspected to be spinal meningitis."[15] Her painful and untimely death at age fifty-six caused the surrounding community to mourn greatly, especially the children who had known her as their Primary President for twenty-five years.[16] Her body was carried home over snowy roads to Bluff by a team of seventeen horses. The whole community turned out to welcome her to her final resting place. "The Indians were in their best native dress and the Primary children clothed in white,"[17] echoing the first apricot blossoms on the trees.

A blessing given to her in 1902 by L. C. Burnham stated: "Your calling and election is made sure, for you shall pass the Celestial Gate . . . Dear sister, how can you mourn when the Lord has given you the power to bring some of the most noble and pure spirits into the world. . . . No woman that was born upon the earth shall have a greater crown and blessing."[18]

NOTES

1. Frances Hoopes, "Josephine Catherine (Jody) Chatterly Wood: Midwife of San Juan. Issue 3, pages 32–41," published as Pioneer History, International Society Daughters of Utah Pioneers. May 12, 2010, 41.

2. Ibid., 32.

3. Ibid.

4. Ibid.

5. Ibid., 33.

6. Ibid.

7. Ibid.

8. Ibid.

9. Ibid.

10. "Journal of Josephine Catherine Chatterly Wood," in "Mormon Midwives," *Utah Historical Quarterly* 10 (1942): 128–36.

11. "Josephine Catherine (Jody) Chatterly Wood: Midwife of San Juan," 35.

12. Ibid., 36.

13. Hansen, Mrs. Lloyd, "Memories of Jody Wood," in *Utah Historical Quarterly* 10 (1942), 128–36.

14. See note 13, and "Mormon Midwives," 133.

15. "Josephine Catherine (Jody) Chatterly Wood: Midwife of San Juan," 42.

16. "Mormon Midwives," 136.

17. "Josephine Catherine (Jody) Chatterly Wood: Midwife of San Juan," 42.

18. Ibid., 41.

LUCY PRATT RUSSELL

March 9, 1848–February 26, 1916

Midwife, mother in her old age, daughter of pioneers,
friend of the poor and downtrodden

L UCY PRATT WAS BORN IN THE OLD FORT IN
Salt Lake City on March 9, 1848, to Parley P. Pratt, Sr., and
Hannaette Snively. She had a childhood filled with hard work
and struggle as the early settlers tried to make a harsh dessert bloom. When
food was scarce, they would eat the bulb of the sego lily. Neighbors would
share soup bones to get two or three boilings out of them.[1] As a young lady,
Lucy served as a schoolteacher,[2] and began her career as a nurse and midwife. She married Samuel Russell on February 14, 1869. The couple longed
for children, and after many years of barrenness, Lucy asked her husband
to take her sister Henrietta to wife as well.[3] When her sister would have
a baby, Lucy would bring the child to bed with her and do all she could
to be a part of the experience. After a blessing from President Joseph F.
Smith, Lucy was able to bear two sons and two daughters. She was seen as
an example of the power of faith.[4] For years, Lucy had helped other women
know the joy of having children, and finally this was hers to know as well.
Lucy also wrote favorable of her experience in being a "sister wife":

> *Now, I would like to ask, has this condition of affairs wrought good or evil?*
> *Those most concerned think the former will far outbalance the latter. Their*
> *greatest ambition was to prove worthy to live in this most Holy and revealed*
> *family order of marriage throughout a never ending eternity. The childless*

one now has four children of her very own. Because their father has gone to the great beyond, she is not as tuneful as of yore and does not always think to sing at eventide, until at their request she sings the same old songs, with the same effect upon her children, bringing back those happy days, not then so full of care.[5]

Lucy had been practicing as a midwife prior to her education by Dr. Romania Pratt in 1878. During the decades of her early youth, being the daughter of polygamous parents posed no difficulty. In the 1880s, however, United States deputies roamed the streets looking for people to arrest and prosecute for living their beliefs. As a consequence of this pressure, many men and women went into hiding or traveled to foreign countries.[6] Midwives and physicians falsified birth records or concealed births.[7] This was occurring at the height of Lucy's practice as a midwife and nurse. She "knew what it meant to dodge the deputies, and since she knew how to deliver a baby without the help of a doctor, she was called hundreds of times to wait upon women who were on the 'underground.'"[8] Lucy and Henrietta raised their children as one big family, with the children referring to them both as mother and aunt. According to her daughter Mrs. Francis B. Platt, Lucy was known for her ability to adapt to any situation as needed. She died on February 26, 1916. [9]

NOTES

1. Russell, Lucy Pratt. *Family Papers, 1837–1937*, Church History Library, MS 418010.
2. Obituary of Lucy Pratt Russell, *Deseret News*, February 26, 1916.
3. Claire Noall, "Mormon Midwives," *Utah Historical Quarterly* 10 (1942), 137.
4. Ibid.
5. Henriette Hope Russell, "A Pioneer History of My Mother Lucy Pratt Russell," submitted to the International Society of Daughters of Utah Pioneers, 4.
6. "Mormon Midwives," 136.
7. Kimberly Jensen James, "'Between Two Fires': Women on the 'Underground' of Mormon Polygamy" (Provo, UT: Brigham Young University Department of History, 1981), 23–35; Kimball Young, *Isn't One Wife Enough?* (Westport, CT: Greenwood Press, 1970), 380–400.
8. "Mormon Midwives," 137.
9. Ibid.

ELLIS REYNOLDS SHIPP

January 20, 1847–January 31, 1939

"I have always tried to do good. I never went to a patient that I didn't go and pray that I might know just what I ought to do before I left home."[1]

"This is our mission, the greatest work that we can perform in this life is to be true wives and faithful mothers."[2]

I N A LOGGING CAMP ON THE BANKS OF A RIVER IN Davis County, Iowa, a baby girl was born just as the sun crested the hills on January 20, 1847. They named her Ellis, for her grandmother.[3] By Ellis's later accounts her early life was extremely happy, with hard working, kind, and industrious parents and grandparents. Her family was stricken by smallpox. Her journals, and poems, record much of her early experiences: *"During those years of hopeful toil and never wavering faith there was born to my parents a precious baby brother— destined not long to remain, for a dreadful scourge of smallpox claimed his precious life! This was my first recollection of sorrow— my stricken parents, a little form carried away in a box. How I wondered, how I cried. I could not comprehend."*[4] Though her father was scarred for life, he was first

to assist others who became ill and acted as a *"friend of the poor, his afflic-tion rendering him immune, and in after years he went about in all epidemics, nursing the victims when no one else had the courage to do so . . . thus he paid his debt of gratitude to Heavenly Father for his own preservation."*[5] Perhaps it was from his example that Ellis learned to visit the sick and afflicted and min-ister to their needs. In 1851, her mother rowed some stranded men across the flooding river close to their cabin. Little did she know that the mes-sage of the restored gospel that they carried would change all of their lives. The whole family was baptized that year and after five years of preparation, made the long wagon trek west to Utah.[6] Ellis writes of these travels:

> *I think my father must have walked the greater part of that long journey! I see him yet, whip in hand but seldom used on his dumb animals, for they seemed to understand his commanding words. My mother with baby brother George in arms, her work in hands, and I close beside her ready to receive the pretty pebbles and shells my father picked up. These wonders of the wilder-ness strewn along nature's highways!*[7]

The whole wagon train was saddened at the passing of Rebecca Winters from cholera, a frequent plague of the time. Ellis writes:

> *One of my most vivid memories on this eventful journey is the death and burial of Rebecca Winters—a lifelong friend and neighbor of my parents. When our dear friend and close neighbor was stricken, my grandmother Ellis Smith Hawley was her constant attendant . . .*
>
> *During those three days of forced encampment in the wilderness, while those sorrowing pilgrims hopelessly awaited the inevitable passing of this pre-cious life, their watchful eyes saw rising dust in the distance, they heard the thud of horse's hooves rapidly approaching and a band of war painted Indians arrived looking threateningly into the faces of the anxious pioneers.*
>
> *The Indians were hungry and demanded food, tobacco and whiskey. After many weeks of travel the supplies of these pilgrims were scarcely suffi-cient for their own needs and they could not relinquish what to them was very life. So they protested and tried to reason with the dark assailants. . . . The company appealed to Captain Hawley [my grandfather], . . . But no. It was food they were determined to have. The captain looked afar quietly and then, turning suddenly, he exclaimed, "Well come on." He led the way to the wagon wherein lay the dying woman. Throwing aside the wagon cover he directed the attention of the savages to the prostrate dying form, in the ghastly pallor of death, eyes wide and sightless. As each one beheld, there was a moment of silence and then there arose deafening yells of fright, and screaming they spurred their animals and flew speedily back from whence they had come.*

Rebecca had saved them, and they honored her memory with a hand-carved wagon wheel placed by the way.[8]

When the family arrived in Salt Lake, they were sent to settle the green valleys of Pleasant Grove. For nearly eight years the family grew and prospered. Ellis had a passion for acquiring knowledge and walked around with her prized dictionary in her dress pocket, pulling it out and pouring over its pages whenever there was a spare moment.[9] Later in life, Ellis would say, *"We cannot give what we do not possess, nor teach what we do not know."*[10] In 1861, Ellis's mother grew weak and ill, finally passing away and leaving fourteen-year-old Ellis with the responsibilities of a household of small children and a grieving father. Her grandparents helped as they could, but this time was extremely difficult for her. *"Never since that hour have I been the carefree child. It was the awakening into responsible womanhood, for I was thus called at the early age of fourteen years to the responsibilities of four younger children, the babe eighteen months—to claim my care. Oh yes, I could work. What solace I found in trying to do as dear mother would be glad to see."*[11] A year later, her father remarried a kind woman, and the family moved to Mount Pleasant, Utah. Ellis spent much of this time with her grandparents. It was here that she was invited by Brigham Young to join his household and receive an education under the renowned German tutor Karl G. Maeser.[12] Young had probably easily recognized Ellis's thirst for knowledge, natural empathy, and work ethic. Ellis lived and studied in the Lion House for about a year. She attended theatre and music hall, and became the friend of Milford Bard Shipp, whom she married on May 5, 1866.[13] She writes, *"The appeal of my soul for a life companion was for one of the highest culture and Godlike intelligence, a mate who could fill my highest ideals of intelligent leadership. . . . My ideal of the union of the sexes I had found in the union of my parents; two hearts that beat as one."*[14] The couple set up house in a tidy home in Salt Lake City and were soon blessed with children. On February 24, 1867, a son was born to Milford and Ellis. She recounts: *"When that tiny precious little body was placed in my arms no mortal pen could tell my joy!"*[15] Shortly after this event, the family relocated to Fillmore to see if Milford's business would thrive there as well. Over the next few years, more children came and the couple knew the sorrow of infant death. Two children, a son and a daughter, would not live long.[16] The couple returned to Salt Lake with three children. Milford returned home to his family and made the announcement that he had accepted the principle of polygamy and that soon a sister wife would join the household.[17] This was especially hard on Ellis, who desperately loved her husband. She relates: *"I had not dreamed this test of faith was so near. Although*

I knew it would be mine in time. I resolved in all humility in my hope and trust and faith to live this principle righteously, even to sharing the love, the attention, the very life of my heart's beloved, with another woman." [18] Ellis, in time, grew to love and cherish her three sister wives. She writes, *"We all lived under the same roof, ate at the same table, knelt at the same shrine, and humbly believed we were doing the will of our Father in Heaven. . . . There still remains after many long years a most sacred bond of fellowship, a beautiful loving interest and sweet affection one for another, that is truly most akin to the divine!"* [19] Indeed, their loving service toward her proved indispensable when she left her children in their care to answer the call to attend medical school. This challenge came when her youngest was still a babe in arms. Her sister wife, Margaret, had returned from medical school unable to complete her studies. (Margaret Curtis Shipp Reynolds would later complete her degree and practice as a physician for many years.) She was asked by Brigham Young to go back East and become a physician to answer the incredible need for care providers, especially in obstetrics. Ellis writes:

> *There are times in our lives when it takes a great deal of courage, some of that old pioneer spirit that was in the hearts of our parents that pioneered across those dreary plains to Utah. It takes a big spark of that spirit to convince a mother that she can leave home and leave her children. I'll never forget how dreadfully I felt. Yet there was an impulse and feeling that I had to go, that I must go, that it would be a blessing to my posterity and the world that I came in contact with. I finally consented to go on very short notice. When I said the last good-byes I can never express how I felt. It was really a great trial to me. But I went to college and I studied very hard, in fact, I was so determined I would succeed that the minute I got on the train and overcame my emotions, I took out my book and began my studies.* [20]

Margaret Curtis Shipp
Reynolds

Ellis studied hard at the Women's Medical College in Philadelphia for a year and was successful. She returned home briefly to Utah over the summer. In the fall, she was destitute of funds, living on bread and milk and newly pregnant with her sixth child. Some of her colleagues advised an abortion, as they stated that she could not possibly

continue through school. Ellis adamantly refused stating, *"Why do you want me to take the life of my own child? I came here to learn how to save life not take it!"*[21] Later in her career, she counseled others: *"I have had many young girls come to me, young girls with no father for their babies and ask, 'Can't you do something? It will mean disgrace for life!' And I have said, 'Girls, you should have thought of this before. Don't do such a thing to those innocent babies. Stand by them, be true to them, take care of them when they come.'"*[22] On May 25, 1878, Ellis bore a baby girl and in June received her degree of doctor of medicine.

Joyously she returned home to Utah and established herself in a separate home with adjoining medical office. The remaining years of Ellis's life are truly remarkable. She traveled from Canada to Mexico training women in the practice of medicine and had over five hundred graduates from her courses. Her School of Obstetrics and Nursing would run continuously until 1938. She delivered over six thousand babies during her fifty-plus-year practice. She states, *"Reverently unto God I give my gratitude for the successful practice of medicine in its many branches for the span of more than fifty years. For more than six thousand times have I felt the exquisite bliss of seeing the mother's smile when for the first time she clasped her treasure in her arms. My specialties in the practice of medicine were obstetrics and the care of women and children."*[23] Ellis bore ten children herself, with four coming after her busy practice was established. Only five would survive to adulthood: Milford Bard (doctor), Richard Asbury (lawyer), Olea S. Hill, Ellis Musser (teacher), and Nellie Shipp McKinley. She served on the General Board of the Relief Society, was a member of the Board of Deseret Hospital, wrote several volumes of poetry,[24] established the first medical journal in Utah,[25] was President of the Utah Women's Press Club and was a delegate to the National Council of Women in Washington, DC.[26] At age ninety she was elected to the Utah Hall of Fame and was honored by her medical school as the oldest practicing physician at that time. She could still be found lecturing on obstetrics shortly before her death on January 31, 1939, at age ninety-two. She would teach her students:

> *When called to maternal duty, pray unto God for His blessing. Pray in your soul as you hasten to your duty. I hastened through inclement storm, through blinding rain, deep snows and muddy trails, speeding up and down the steepest hills, my inmost being pulsating with fervent prayer. I sought my Father and my God! He it was who inspired me with higher intelligence, helped me to know my duty in all of its details, enabled me to run and not be weary, to walk and not faint. And with these same principles I tutored all who sought usefulness, enabling them to usher a new life into this world—*

that life so precious to the suffering mother and most sublime in the sight of God.[27]

Her life was exemplified by service and devotion to her faith. She longed for the unity of mankind. One of her poems states: "Will not there come a time when but one creed there'll be?/ When all shall come to one great shrine, with bended knee,/ With contrite, humble heart, with pliant yielding will,/ All seeking for the truth, God's purpose to fulfill? And should we not as children of the same great Sire,/ Have but one Lord, one Faith, one great and good desire?"[28] Her legacy lives on in the free health clinic named for her in West Valley City, Utah, a shadow of the free maternity hospital she envisioned on Ensign Peak.[29] It speaks through the generations of women she empowered to serve each other. It whispers each time a newborn draws its first breath beneath the towering Rocky Mountains.

NOTES

1. Ellis Reynolds Shipp, talk given to Daughters of Utah Pioneers, Camp Nine, Salt Lake City, UT, June 1832, 9.

2. Ibid.

3. Ellis Reynolds Shipp, *Autobiography of Ellis Reynolds Shipp M.D.*, 1961, compiled by Ellis Shipp Musser (Salt Lake City, Utah), 5.

4. Ibid., 2.

5. Ibid., 2.

6. Winston B. Shipp, *Women of Faith and Fortitude: Ellis Reynolds Shipp, submitted to Daughters of Utah Pioneers, 1982* Salt Lake City: Daughters of Utah Pioneers., 1982), 1

7. *Autobiography of Ellis Reynolds Shipp M.D.*, 3.

8. Ibid., 5–7.

9. Ibid., 16

10. Ibid., 54.

11. Ibid., 20.

12. *Women of Faith and Fortitude: Ellis Reynolds Shipp*, 1.

13. Ibid.

14. *Autobiography of Ellis Reynolds Shipp M.D.,,* 29.

15. Ibid., 39.

16. *Women of Faith and Fortitude: Ellis Reynolds Shipp*, , 2.

17. Ibid., 1.

18. *Autobiography of Ellis Reynolds Shipp M.D.*, 42.

19. Ibid., 59.

absent ZION'S HOPE

20. Ellis Reynolds Shipp, talk given to Daughters of Utah Pioneers, Camp Nine, Salt Lake City, UT, June 1832, 5.

21. Ibid., 7.

22. Ibid., 8.

23. *Autobiography of Ellis Reynolds Shipp M.D.*, 53.

24. Ellis Reynolds Shipp, *Life Lines–Poems* (Salt Lake City: Skelton Publishing Company, 1910).

25. *Women of Faith and Fortitude: Ellis Reynolds Shipp*, 9.

26. Blanche E. Rose, "Early Utah Medical Practice: Women Doctors" *Utah Historical Quarterly* 10 (1942), 31.

27. *Autobiography of Ellis Reynolds Shipp M.D.*, 54.

28. *Women of Faith and Fortitude: Ellis Reynolds Shipp*.

29. Ellis R. Shipp Public Health Center: 4535 South 5600 West, West Valley City, Utah 84120.

JANE WILKIE
MANNING SKOLFIELD

May 19, 1866–February 11, 1935

"Happy is the man who has found his work."[1]

O N MAY 19, 1866, A BABY GIRL WAS BORN TO
Henry William and Margaret Galbraith Manning on a small
farm in Weber County, Utah. They named her Jane Wilkie and
she was the sixth of ten children. Her father was a skilled cabinetmaker
from England and worked hard to support his family. At the age of three,
Jane moved with her family to a nicer
farm in Hooper. Her father became
the postmaster and owner of a general store. As Jane grew, she helped
her father sort the mail and keep the
books.[2] Love blossomed in her life at
the age of nineteen, and a marriage
to Jedidiah Ballantyne soon followed.
Newly married, Jane was left to support herself and her first baby, Jennie,
while Jedidiah served a mission for the
Church. Jane used her keen mind to
secure a local teaching position. In the
mornings, she would ride "three miles
on horseback . . . to leave the baby,

with her sister Mary, and at noon [would ride] back to nurse [her infant]."[3]
Jedidiah returned, but "when her second child, Mazel . . . was two years old,
[Jane] was left a widow."[4] Again she used her skills to support her family of
three. She gathered several local women and set up a successful dressmak-
ing shop. Forward thinking, she began taking classes at Weber Academy,
eventually transferring to Brigham Young Academy. She graduated with a
degree in kindergarten (early childhood education) in 1895. She then fur-
thered her education at the Chicago Kindergarten College and the Mother's
Kindergarten Work in New York. She eventually became the supervisor of
the kindergarten department at Brigham Young Academy and served as a
delegate to the International Kindergarten Union.[5]

Jane later married Samuel Reed Skolfield and worked hard to help
establish a branch of the LDS Church in Denver, Colorado. She also joined
the Denver Philosophical Society. She returned home to Utah in 1899
to have a third child and had a fourth child, Elizabeth, in 1902. When
tiny Elizabeth was six weeks old, Jane entered the Denver and Gross Medical College. Her oldest daughter watched the children during the day and
brought the baby to school at lunch for a feeding. During vacations and holi-
days, Jane would attend obstetrical cases to earn money for tuition. During
her junior year, however, Jane had to drop out of school to nurse her children who had contracted whooping cough and typhoid fever. She returned
to school and doubled her efforts.

Triumphantly, Jane graduated from medical school on May 16, 1907.
The family moved back to Salt Lake City, and Jane began her employment
with the LDS Hospital as the first female intern admitted to any Utah hospital staff. She remained an active part of this facility for over twenty-five
years, and acted as the examining physician for graduating nursing classes.
She also worked at Holy Cross Hospital (now Salt Lake Regional) and was
beloved of the nuns. Jane was a member of the Utah Mental Health Association, the American Medical Association, and the Utah State Medical
Association. Jane was extremely active in public life, guest lecturing many
times a month, and serving as a delegate to the First National Health Con-
vention and Chairman of Sanitation for the City Civics Club. She also acted
as President of the Utah Women's Press Club for two years. Most notably,
"Dr. Jane" was elected to the State Legislature where she successfully passed
bills on eugenics and establishing a minimum wage for women. In her medical practice, Jane strongly encouraged unwed mothers to keep their infants.[6]
She was an advocate for health care to the poor, as were Dr. Ellis Shipp and
Dr. Margaret Shipp, her contemporaries. She wanted women to rise up in

their communities and make a difference in the cause of family. At a conference, she elaborated upon these ideas:

> *Women can become mighty factors in the cause of peace. It is her hand that can rule the world if she will . . . she is the first teacher of the young, and she can mold the spirit of peace. Our children should be familiar with what is going on in the world today, they should be taught concerning the causes of war, the awful destruction of human life.*
>
> *The women of our nation have been traditionally true; they have stood the test. In behalf of the women of the peace committee of the whole nation I feel I can vouch that whatever movement may be made throughout the world today we will stand heart in hand ready to do all that we shall be called upon to do.*[7]

Jane delivered over three thousand babies, the last case being that of the Nielsen triplets in Sandy, Utah. Jane pushed herself to achieve relentlessly. This intensity led to her suffering a hemorrhagic stroke on March 1, 1932. Reduced to life in a wheelchair and the end of her many activities, she sadly lamented, *"But I could never foresee a time . . . that I couldn't go on, and there is so much to be done."*[8] Jane struggled for three more years in this state, passing away on February 11, 1935. She is buried in the Wasatch Cemetery. The quote that hung above her desk during her medical career explains her drive to do good while she had breath, "Happy is the man who has found his work."[9]

NOTES

1.   Jennie Skolfield, "History of My Mother Jane Wilkie Manning Skolfield," archived by the International Society of Daughters of Utah Pioneers, 1959, 1.
2.   Ibid.
3.   Ibid.
4.   Ibid.
5.   Ibid.
6.   Ibid., 2–5
7.   Ibid., 3.
8.   Ibid., 5.
9.   Ibid., 1.

PERSIS YOUNG RICHARDS

July 2, 1864–August 28, 1901

Midwife though heartbreakingly childless herself,
conspirator, faithful Saint

PERSIS YOUNG WAS BORN JULY 2, 1864, AND raised in St. Charles, Idaho. Her father Franklin W. Young had later been called to settle Fruita, Utah. Persis spent her teen years working in Salt Lake City as a nurse.[1] She showed an early aptitude for this work and was soon caring for those recovering on her own.[2] She came to be in the employ of the Richards family when Lulu took to child-bed. Persis cared for Lulu, the infant, and her three small sons. Later, Levi asked Persis to become his second wife. At this time, federal pressure to stop polygamy was gaining momentum, and Levi asked Persis's parents to come and take her home to Fruita while she was expecting.[3] The trip was an arduous 255 miles by wagon, and the winter weather was harsh. A blizzard approached and the team of horses was having great difficulty pulling up the steep mountain pass. The road was narrow, with a drop off down into a canyon. The horses slipped and the

sled began to fall over the edge. All occupants were jarred and tossed about. A rescue party soon arrived to guide them the rest of the way home. Persis was in trouble, though. The accident had damaged her unborn baby, who was stillborn after a difficult delivery. Persis would never be able to bear another child.[4] This grieved her heart, but in the true spirit of charity, she used her pain to motivate her to study how to save others. Persis returned to Salt Lake and began study with Dr. Ellis R. Shipp. She graduated and began to practice in Salt Lake. She related how she and other midwives actively conspired against the authorities seeking to discover and prosecute those practicing polygamy. This was prior to the Manifesto, when the small majority of Saints practicing polygamy believed they were following the will of God and that they were bound to a higher law. Persis tells how *"one baby had to be carried from its mother after the first suckling because the United States deputies were prowling about the house. She wrapped him up and in the dead of night took him in a buggy away from the house where the mother had been confined. On another occasion, the mother was moved almost immediately after her baby was born."*[5]

Persis loved the work of midwife and nurse. She died on August 28, 1901.

NOTES

1. Claire Noall, "Mormon Midwives," *Utah Historical Quarterly* 10 (1942): 137.
2. Ibid., 137.
3. Ibid., 138.
4. Ibid.
5. Ibid.

MARGERY LISK SPENCE

February 18, 1811–December 30, 1882

Scottish convert, nurse during the Crimean War, mother, midwife

ORN ON THE SHETLAND ISLANDS OFF THE coast of Scotland on February 18, 1811, Margery Lisk would serve a community nearly three thousand miles away until her passing at age seventy-one. Both her father and later her husband were sailors and shipbuilders. After her father was drowned at sea, the family moved to London. Her husband was lost at sea and presumed dead, so Margery looked for ways to support her family. (Two years later, he would find his way home, but was permanently injured from his trial.) Margery was introduced to the Church while nursing soldiers wounded in the Crimean War in London. Little is known about this period, though her daughter Emma would grow to marry Thomas Ellerbeck, secretary to Brigham Young. After some time, the couple sent money back to England for the passage of Margery and her son Will. They arrived in Salt Lake City on September 3, 1866.[1] The remainder of the family soon followed. Margery went to work as a nurse and midwife. Margery, though small and dainty, spent her time caring for others, including her invalid husband, John, a retired sea captain.[2] Her obituary reads: "Sister Spence was well known in nearly every part of the city as a skillful and successful nurse, ready at any hour of the day or night to attend those in need of her services. She was ever affable, patient and kind and very successful in cases of [childbirth]. She will be affectionately remembered by a host of ladies who were blessed by her presence and attention during the trying hours [of giving birth]."[3]

NOTES

1.   Claire Noall, "Mormon Midwives," *Utah Historical Quarterly* 10 (1942): 114.
2.   Ibid., 115.
3.   *Deseret News*, "Obituary of Margery Spence," January 3, 1882. Archived.

MARY ANN SWENSON

August 15, 1868–March 23, 1937

"Don't be afraid dear. All this is so natural there is nothing to be frightened of."[1]

MARY ANN SWENSON WAS BORN IN SALT Lake City on August 15, 1868. Little is written about her early years, but we do know she actively served as a nurse both before and after her marriage to Mr. Swenson, a carpenter by trade. When Mary was thirty and all but four of her children grown, the family moved to Driggs, Idaho, a beautiful hamlet on the western side of the Teton Range. Here the family learned that the soil was too poor and the climate too harsh to raise many crops. Mary's husband continued in carpentry to support the family and Mary continued her nursing.[2] When Dr. Ellis R. Shipp traveled through the area to start classes in obstetrics, Mary seized the opportunity. Studying hard, she graduated one year later with her certificate and gave birth to her last child.[3] Mary became the midwife and doctor to the surrounding area, charging $2.50 for ten days of care if the family could afford to pay, and nothing if they could not.[4] Her preteen daughter Lorinda assumed much of the household duties when her mother was away on a case.[5] Mary was well acquainted with the power of prayer. Once Lorinda came upon her mother in her bedroom thanking her Father in Heaven for saving the life of a mother whom she had despaired over saving. Mary attributes her son's recovery from a near-fatal case of peritonitis to her prayers on his behalf.[6] She always prayed to know what to do prior to leaving on a case. The family later moved to Twin Falls to enjoy

the milder climate, where Mary would practice her art for eighteen more years. The area had plenty of physicians who initially scoffed at her skills, but quickly gained respect and even admiration for her.[7] Mary kept up her deliveries until five years before her death on March 23, 1937. [8]

NOTES

1.   Claire Noall, "Mormon Midwives," *Utah Historical Quarterly* 10 (1942): 143–44.

2.   Ibid., 142.

3.   Ibid., 143.

4.   Ibid., 144

5.   Ibid., 143.

6.   Ibid.

7.   Ibid., 144.

8.   Ibid.

VIGDIS BJORNSDOTTIR HOLT

April 27, 1824–December 2, 1913

*Physician to Spanish Fork, one of the first
converts from Iceland, shepherdess*

TINY GIRL WAS BORN ON THE FARAWAY
shores of Iceland on April 27, 1824, to Bjorn Gislason and
Hildur Filippusdottir. They named her Vigdis (Vickie), and
though small in stature with light brown hair and blue eyes, she had a sharp
mind and cheerful spirit. As a young woman, Vigdis left her native home
to travel to Denmark and pursue the study of medicine.[1] Graduating as a
physician, she returned home to begin her work. At this point she was introduced to the Church and became one of the first converts in Iceland. She
was baptized on May 27, 1855, at the age of thirty-one. Her mother would
pass away a few months later in September. Three years later, her father
would also die. Vigdis longed to be with the Saints in Zion and so she left
her practice and sailed for America. She settled in Spanish Fork, Utah, and
had the comfort of having a small Icelandic community around her.[2] She fell
in love with William Holt and was married to him on April 14, 1861. Vigdis
served her community as doctor, midwife, and nurse. She was known as
"Aunt Wickie Holt" or "Grandma Holt." She set bones, treated myriad illnesses, and delivered several hundred babies. She was still riding horseback
to cases with her satchel tied securely to the saddle at the age of eighty. She
also kept sheep and would spin and weave her own clothing from their wool.

Sometimes she would take wool with her to impoverished families as she treated their health issues.[3] Her neighbors related: "We loved her because of her noble, self-sacrificing character, her undaunted faith and her love for those whose life did not hold an overflowing cup of happiness. [She] was one of those who thought little of herself, but was always ready to do a kind and obliging deed for another. We shall always remember her noble character."[4] Dr. Holt passed away at the age of eighty-nine years on December 2, 1913. She is buried in the Spanish Fork Cemetery.

NOTES

1.   Icelandic Settlers of Utah, "Vigdis Bjornsdottir," accessed February 22, 2011, www.tahicelandersdavid.com.

2.   Ibid.

3.   Ibid.

4.   Ibid.

MARTHA HUGHES
PAUL CANNON

July 1, 1857–July 10, 1932

*"You give me a woman who thinks about something besides
cook stoves and wash tubs and baby flannels, and I'll show you,
nine times out of ten, a successful mother."*[1]

ARTHA MARIE HUGHES WAS BORN TO
Peter and Elizabeth Hughes in Llandudno, Wales, on
July 1, 1857. She was the second of three girls. Peter was
a cabinetmaker by trade, and in the course of his business, the family was
introduced to the missionaries of The
Church of Jesus Christ of Latter-day
Saints. Though her father was weak and
suffered from chronic illness, the family
strongly desired to come to America.
They sailed toward their new land on
March 30, 1860. Peter was too weak to
travel beyond New York, so Elizabeth
went to work to support the family. After
three long years, Peter was no better and
the decision was made to cross the plains
immediately in the hope that Peter might
live to at least see his new home.[2] Along
the way, little four-month-old Annie

passed away and was buried in an unmarked grave by the way. Three days after reaching the Salt Lake Valley, Peter succumbed to his illness and died.[3] Martha was only four years old and had already experienced things which would mold her future course. The family settled into their new home and one year later, Elizabeth remarried a widower named James Patton Paul, who was raising four boys from his first marriage.[4] Martha could not have been blessed by a better stepfather. "Father Paul" lovingly raised Martha to believe that she could accomplish anything.[5] Noticing her keen mind, he made sure she had an education, and in later years would do all he could to financially support her medical schooling. To help with the support of family, Martha began teaching school at the age of fourteen.[6] Brigham Young called her to be a typesetter for the *Deseret Evening News* and the *Women's Exponent*.[7] She also learned Swedish in order to make extra money printing in that language. Martha was happy in her work, but not content. She had always been distressed by illness and longed to help improve the conditions of those living around her.[8] She decided to enroll at Deseret University (now the University of Utah) and take pre-medical courses. The University of Michigan at Ann Arbor had recently opened enrollment to women, and after three years of difficult study, poor food, and long days, Martha graduated with her medical degree on her twenty-third birthday.[9] That summer she enrolled in two additional programs in Pennsylvania: the School of Elocution and Oratory[10] and the School of Pharmacy.[11] Martha knew she would need additional skills if she were to truly reshape her community for the better.

After four years, having obtained three degrees, Martha returned home and opened a small medical practice. Once again, her stepfather demonstrated his support by building another wing of the family home for a medical suite. Martha soon gained an excellent reputation and was asked to be the second resident physician at Deseret Hospital. She worked hard there for three years,[12] performing surgeries, teaching, providing obstetrical care, and doing many other tasks.[13] She was extremely devoted to the notion of hygiene and its relationship to health. In fact, it was while she was mopping the front steps of the hospital that she met her soon-to-be husband, Angus M. Cannon, president of the Salt Lake Stake and hospital superintendent. As he was tromping up her freshly cleaned portico, she sternly asked him to step away and choose another path. Angus was indignant that a "mopping girl" would order him around. Martha would not back down and Angus had to acquiesce. Later as he was inspecting the hospital, he saw this same woman preparing to perform a surgery. He entered the room to speak with

her and again she asked him to leave, being concerned with the spread of germs.[14] These two encounters left their mark on Angus, and Martha was married to him on October 6, 1884,[15] becoming his fourth wife. Due to the anti-polygamy laws being enacted by Congress at the time, Martha and Angus kept their union a secret even from family members until Martha's first child, Elizabeth, was born one year later.[16] Martha was on her own as Angus had been sentenced to six months in the Sugar House Prison for "Cohabitation," or the practice of polygamy.[17] Martha was hidden in Grantsville with friends. She moved to Centerville, traveling under hay in the back of a wagon with her tiny four-month-old. The experience shook Martha as her baby was near frozen upon arrival. She decided to leave America and travel to stay with relatives in England.[18] She wrote to Angus: "*I would rather be a stranger in a strange land and be able to hold my head up among my fellow beings than to be a sneaking captive at home.*"[19] She initially found welcome in her uncle's household, lecturing at local hospitals and learning new techniques as she could. Her family later denied her hospitality when her relationship with Angus became known.[20] Exile was very difficult for Martha, and she wrote to Angus of her eagerness to return: "*The gallant ship is under weigh/ To bear us off to sea./ And yonder floats the streamers gay/ That says she waits for "we"/ The seamen dip the ready oar/ As rippling waves oft tell/ They bear us swiftly from the shore/ Our native land farewell/ Everything is lovely and the goose hangs high.*"[21] Sometimes she would refer to herself as the "*Bitter, Rebellious, Star of the Sea.*"[22] She spoke of her loneliness, "*There was a time in my life when letters were a burden, you could never imagine my situation unless you were here. I'm beginning to realize how dear you are to me.*"[23] Despite the hardships of being a polygamous wife in a time of persecution, Martha stated shortly before her return to Utah: "*Hence I am considered an important witness, and if it can be proven that these children have actually come into the world, their fathers will be sent to jail for five (5) years. . . . To me it is a serious matter to be the cause of sending to jail a father upon whom a lot of little children are dependent, whether those children were begotten by the same or different mothers—the fact remains they all have little mouths that must be fed.*"[24] Two years later, the couple reunited. Angus had built Martha a home, and she resumed the practice of medicine. Their son James was born May 17, 1890, and two months later, the Manifesto ending polygamy was signed, after which Martha became heavily involved in the suffrage movement. Martha saw polygamy as liberation for women of that day: "*If her husband has four wives, she has three weeks of freedom every single month.*"[25] This activity merged her innate desire to improve conditions of

the weaker and more vulnerable players in Victorian society with her long experience in health care and reform. She was active in representing the women of Utah on a national level. Fate drove her to run for public office on the Democratic ticket in 1896. Defeating her husband and six others running for the same seat by four thousand votes, Martha became the first female senator in Utah. During her time as a senator, she was successful in passing legislation that still has a far-reaching impact on the people of Utah. Martha established compulsory education for deaf, dumb, and blind children, created a State Board of Health, and passed legislation to protect and establish minimum wages for female workers.[26] Martha bore a third child, Gwendolyn, to Angus three weeks after the 1899 session ended. During her service in the next term, Martha sponsored further public health laws, some of which remain in place to this day and govern regulation of infectious diseases, animal disease control, food inspection, and vital statistics tracking. Though Martha was extremely active in public life, her children speak strongly of her love and devotion for them. In the early 1900s, she began to suffer from poor health and moved her medical practice to California. She did mostly volunteer work at the Orthopedic Department of Grave's Medical Clinic and was considered an authority on narcotics addiction. She worked until the age of seventy-four, when she was diagnosed with terminal cancer. She passed away on July 10, 1932, and was asked to be buried next to Angus in Salt Lake City, Utah.[27] The current State Department of Health building in Utah is named for her, and a large statue of her created by sculptor Laura Lee Stay at the state capitol marks her significant life.[28]

NOTES

1. Constance L. Lieber and John Sillito, eds. *Letters from Exile: The Correspondence of Martha Hughes Cannon and Angus M. Cannon, 1886–1888* (Salt Lake City: Signature Books, 1993).

2. Gloria Alsop, *Women of Faith and Fortitude: Martha Maria Hughes Canon*, archived by Daughters of Utah Pioneers, unknown date, 2–3.

3. Blanche E. Rose, "Early Utah Medical Practice: Women Doctors," *Utah Historical Quarterly* 10 (1942), 30.

4. *Women of Faith and Fortitude: Martha Maria Hughes Canon*, 2–3.

5. Ibid.

6. Ibid.

7. Dennis Lythgoe, "Physician/plural wife was real pioneer in women's rights," *Deseret News*, March 3, 1991.

Z I O N ' S   H O P E

8. *Women of Faith and Fortitude: Martha Maria Hughes Canon*, 2–3.

9. Ibid.

10. "Early Utah Medical Practice: Women Doctors," 30.

11. Schricker, J. Louis, Jr., M.D. F.A.C.S., *Martha Hughes Cannon* (International Society of Daughters of Utah Pioneers, unknown date), 1–7.

12. Ibid.

13. "Early Utah Medical Practice: Women Doctors," 30.

14. *Martha Hughes Cannon*, 1–7.

15. "Early Utah Medical Practice: Women Doctors," 30.

16. Ibid.

17. *Letters from Exile*, xv.

18. *Martha Hughes Cannon*, 1–7.

19. *Letters from Exile*, 269.

20. "Early Utah Medical Practice: Women Doctors," 30.

21. Elizabeth Cannon McCrimmon, *Dr. Martha Hughes Cannon, Journal Entry*, Daughters of Utah Pioneers Archives, 1944, 1–4.

22. *Letters from Exile*.

23. *Letters from Exile*.

24. MHC to Barbara Reployle, 21 March 185, MHC, HDC. In ibid., xv.

25. Dennis Lythgoe, Physician/Plural Wife Was Real Pioneer in Women's Rights," *Deseret News*, March 3, 1991.

26. *Martha Hughes Cannon*.

27. *Martha Hughes Cannon*, 7.

28. Harold Schindler, "Sculptor's Subject a Tall Order," *Salt Lake Tribune*, July 16, 1995.

APPENDIX I

OTHER NOTABLE PROVIDERS

ANY OTHER WOMEN SERVED AS FAITHFUL
midwives and doctors in the communities of Utah, Idaho,
and surrounding areas. Though just as worthy of mention,
their stories were beyond the scope of this work. We must remember that
at the time, midwifery was a stake calling in the Church and so three or
more women would be called per stake to assist in the work of bringing
forth new life. The walls in the Pioneer Midwife room of the Museum of
the International Daughters of Utah Pioneers are peppered with black-
and-white photos of these women. They are listed here in case the reader
desires to study further, with dates of birth and death if available: Janet
Downie Hardie, Almena Randall Farr, Eliza Wesley, Margaret Galbraith
Manning, Augustus Dorius Stevens, Jane Patterson Brough, Hannah
Maria Aylett, Mary Argent, Margaret Maria Sorenson Edwards (February 17, 1860–April 12, 1946), Georgina Kjoller Ipson, Mary E. S. Porter
(b. October 23, 1858), Anne C. Hansen, Ruth Sweetnam Talbot (February 4, 1817–March 15, 1903), Elizabeth Durrah Wilkins, Patience Delilah Pierce Palmer (February 15, 1809–March 25, 1894), Anna Cutler
Galloway (April 5, 1831–August 2, 1895), Olive Ann Johnsen String-
ham (May 9, 1862–December 1939), Hulda Dimeras Vaughn Harmon
Bassett (February 11, 1808–October 12, 1886), Pauly Chapman Bybee
Hammon (October 28, 1820–August 7, 1902), Maria Johnston Wood-
ward (October 28, 1824–February 14, 1911), Hulda T. Smith, Sabra

Jane Beckstead Hatch (October 20, 1853–10 May 1946), Sarah Farr Le Cheminant (February 24, 1813–July 19, 1901), Mary H. McAllister, Elizabeth H. Shaw, Janet J. Smith, Mary B. Schurtz, Mary Frances Barnett Reynolds (October 17, 1838–July 21, 1921), Leah Jane Shaw Keeler (September 17, 1851–December 17, 1936), Ann Hess Milne (March 8, 1854–October 10, 1921), Elizabeth Birch Harker (April 4, 1830–November 23, 1897), Gerusha Hambleton Boswell, Regula Benz Naegle (July 1, 1839–October 20, 1921), Sarah T. S. Black, Frances E. Jones Bridges, Sarah Jane Veach Lewis (October 26, 1834–March 2, 1913), Caroline A. Mills (1860–1933), Catherine Foy Blackburn, L. Christina Nielsen Larsen (October 23, 1833–July 2, 1921), Lucinda Patten (November 19, 1859–December 4, 1923), Johanne Christine Handberg Nicol, Margaret Bowman Duncan (April 5, 1822–July 22, 1904), Sarah E. Ashworth Sears (September 10, 1864–22 January 1935), Permilla H. Swain, Louis O'Bray Gibbs, Martha Ann Bingham (February 20, 1833–November 18, 1898), Margaret McCleave Hancock (September 17, 1838–May 4, 1908), Mary Swindle, Mary Nebecker, Elizabeth Fife Blair, Jane Meredith Simons (July 23, 1826–May 2, 1897), Elizabeth Rodwell (September 22, 1805–October 5, 1882), Sarah M. C. Tyson (April 5, 1841–August 20, 1920), Harriet D. Johnson (March 12, 1805–January 16, 1883), Mary Ann Gibson (December 23, 1823–September 3, 1888), Jane Muday Andrus (October 4, 1832–October 2, 1900), Nancy Elenor Hall (March 2, 1819–March 11, 1889), Margaret Evans Pryor, Matilda Swenson (May 8, 1845–October 17, 1928), Ellen Galleger Cottam, Hannah Blench Pidcock (September 11, 1832–January 20, 1898), Mary Pass Burton (July 28, 1951–August 31, 1931), Henrietta McKay McCloy (November 24, 1842–December 23, 1902), Livinia Ann Wall (April 27, 1837–March 1, 1901), Sarah Finley Hardy (February 18, 1819–February 2, 1901), Elizabeth Winchester (February 11, 1833–March 7, 1920), Mary Ann Hale Johnson (August 11, 1826–December 17, 1911), Adaline Knight Belnap (May 4, 1831–June 10, 1919), Julia Clark Harrington (March 7, 1803–October 6, 1886), Sarah Simmons Warren (July 8, 1840–September 14, 1918), Mary F. A. Merell, Sarah Finley Merrell.

REFERENCES

Maureen Ursenbach Beecher, "'All Things move in Order in the City': the Nauvoo Diary of Zina Diantha Huntington Jacobs," *BYU Studies Quarterly* 19, no. 3 (Provo, UT: Brigham Young University Press, 1979).

Arrington, Leonard J., and David Bitton. *The Mormon Experience: A History of the Latter-day Saints*. Urbana: Univeristy of Illinois Press, 1992.

Atchley, Tom. *Early Black History of the San Bernadino Valley*. San Bernadino: San Bernadino Commemoration edition, 1974.

Beasley, Delilah L. *The Negro Trail Blazers of California*. G.K. Hall and Co., 1998.

Beller, Jack. "Negro Slaves in Utah." *Utah Historical Quarterly* 2 (October 1924): 122–26.

Berwanger, Eugene H. *The Frontier Against Slavery: Western Anti-Negro Prejudice and the Slavery Extension Controversy*. Urbana: University of Illinois Press, 1967.

Bevan, Lucille M. *"History of Emma Batchelor."* Submitted manuscript to the International Society of Daughters of Utah Pioneers, archived 1945.

Bitton, Davis. *Guide to Mormon Diaries and Autobiographies*. Provo: Brigham Young University Press, 1977.

Bolden, Tonya. *The Book of African-American Women: 150 Crusaders, Creators and Uplifters*. Adams Media Corp., 1996.

"The Bridget 'Biddy' Mason Case" (1856) http://www.blackpast.org.

Bringhurst, Newell G. *Saints, Slaves and Blacks: The Changing Place of Blacks within Mormonism*. Westport, CT: Greenwood, 1981.

Brooks, Juanita, ed. *On the Mormon Frontier: The Diary of Hosea Stout*. 2 vols. Salt Lake City: University of Utah Press, 1964.

Bukke, Inger. "Stories from Your Museum, March Lesson: Hilda Andersson Erickson." Submitted to International Society Daughters of Utah Pioneers, n.d., 1.

Burbank, Sarah S. *Autobiographical Sketch, 1924*, Church History Library, MS 3039.

Bush, Lester E., Jr., and Armand L. Mauss, eds. *Neither White nor Black: Mormon Scholars Confront the Race Issue in a Universal Church*. Midvale, Utah: Signature Books, 1984.

Campbell, Catherine Wright. "Biography of Annie Bryceon Laker." Archived by the International Society of Utah Pioneers, May 21, 1997.

Campbell, Eugene. "A History of the Church of Jesus Christ of Latter-day Saints in California." PhD diss., University of Southern California, 1952.

Carter, Kate B. "Eliza Marie Patridge Lyman." In *Treasures of Pioneer History*, ed. Kate B. Carter, 12:213–84. Salt Lake City: Daughters of the Utah Pioneers, 1953.

———. *Heart Throbs of the West*, vol. 2, ed., Kate B. Carter. (Salt Lake City: Daughters of Utah Pioneers, 1951).

———. *The Story of the Negro Pioneer*. Salt Lake City: Daughters of the Utah Pioneers, 1965.

Casto, Alice B. *Memories of Grandma Andrus*. Submitted to International Society of Daughters of Utah Pioneers, 1944.

Coleman, Ronald G. "A History of Blacks in Utah, 1825–1910." PhD diss., University of Utah, 1980.

Commire, Anne, ed. *Women in World History: A Biographical Encyclopedia.* Waterford, CT: Yorkin Publications, 1999.

Cook, Alonzo Laker. *Memories of My Grandmother.* Daughters of Utah Pioneers International, February 26, 1934.

Cook, Melvin A. *Autobiography of Melvin A Cook, Volume One: Reflections on Ancestry and Early Life.* Daughters of Utah Pioneers International.

Daurelle, Jude. "Buckskin, Lace and Forceps: Hilda A. Erickson, Utah Pioneer." *Piecework*, November/December, 43–51. 1993.

Demaratus, De Etta. *The Force of a Feather: The Search for a Lost Story of Slavery and Freedom.* Salt Lake City: University of Utah Press, 2002.

Deseret News. "Obituary of Catherine Mary Oldroyd," April 10, 1897.

———. "Obituary of Margery Spence," January 3, 1882. Archived.

———. "Obituary of Phebe Amelia Richards Pert," January 16, 1943.

Drumiler, Daniel. *Anna Regula Furrer, Life History.* Presented August 9, 1997, Philippe Cardon Reunion.

Erickson, Hilda. *Journal.* Archived by International Society of Daughters of Utah Pioneers.

Ferris, Jeri Chase. *With Open Hands: A Story About Biddy Mason.* Minneapolis: Carolrhoda Books, 2002.

Gates, Susa Young. *History of the Young Ladies' Mutual Improvement Association of the Church of Jesus Christ of Latter-day Saints from November 1869 to June 1910.* Salt Lake City: *Deseret News*, 1911. In "Centennial of President Zina D. H. Young," *Relief Society Magazine* 8, no. 3 (March 1921), 133.

Geisler, Pat M. *Women of Faith and Fortitude—Harriet Sanders Kimball.* Heber C Kimball Family Association, archived by the International Society of Daughters of Utah Pioneers, 1976.

Goode, Kenneth G. *California's Black Pioneers: A Brief Historical Survey.* Santa Barbara: McNally and Loftin, 1974.

Greenhalgh, Franklin. Letter. Published in *Utah Historical Quarterly* 10 (1942): 123.

Halliday, Maragret H. "Sarah Southworth Burbank," www.rawlins.org.

Hansen, Mrs. Lloyd. "Memories of Jody Wood," in *Utah Historical Quarterly* 10 (1942): 128–36.

Hayden, Dolores. "Biddy Mason's Los Angeles, 1856–1891." *California History* 68, no. 3 (1989): 99.

Hayes, Benjamin. *Pioneer Notes from the Diaries of Judge Benjamin Hayes, 1849–1875.* Ed. Marjorie Tisdale Wolcott. Los Angeles: n.p., 1929.

Hine, Darlene Clark, ed., *Black Women in America: An Historical Encyclopedia*, Brooklyn, NY: Carlson Publishing, 1993.

Hoopes, Frances. *Josephine Catherine (Jody) Chatterly Wood: Midwife of San Juan.* Published as Pioneer History, International Society Daughters of Utah Pioneers. May 12, 2010. Issue 3, 32–41.

Icelandic Settlers of Utah. "Vigdis Bjornsdottir," accessed February 22, 2011, www.tahicelandersdavid.com.

International Society of Daughters of Utah Pioneers. *Pioneer Women of Faith and Fortitude.* Various authors. Compiled and submitted, 1998.

James, Kimberly Jensen, "'Between Two Fires': Women on the 'Underground' of Mormon Polygamy" (Provo, UT: Brigham Young University Department of History, 1981).

Jenson, Andrew. *Encyclopedic History of the Church of Jesus Christ of Latter-day Saints.* Salt Lake City: *Deseret News*, 1941.

———. *Latter-day Saint Biographical Encyclopedia*, vol. 4. (Salt Lake City, UT: *Deseret News*, 1943), 193.

Jenson, Harold H. "Utah's Last Pioneer." *Salt Lake Tribune*, November 1, 1964.

Journal of Sarah Southworth Burbank. LDS Church Historical Archives, accepted 1950.

King, Laura, and P. Angell. "Women of the Mormon Battalion and Mississippi Saints." In *Heart Throbs of the West*, vol. 2, ed., Kate B. Carter. Salt Lake City: Daughters of Utah Pioneers, 1951, 65–87.

Klemke, Edith and Bob Weed. *Robert Mays Smith: From South Carolina to Texas (the Long way)*. Wolfe City, TX: Hennington, 1988.

Laker, Annie Bryceon. "Memories." Submitted by grandson Alonzo Laker Cook. Archived by International Daughters of Utah Pioneers, February 26, 1934.

Lambson, Julina. *Journal*, archived by International Society of Daughters of Utah Pioneers.

Larn, Hubert. "Fantastic Hilda: Pioneer History Personified. *Swedish Historical Society Quarterly* (June 1964).

Lieber, Constance L., and John Sillito, eds. *Letters from Exile: The Correspondence of Martha Hughes Cannon and Angus M. Cannon, 1886–1888*. Salt Lake City: Signature Books, 1993.

Lyman, Albert R. *Amasa Mason Lyman: Trailblazer and Pioneer from the Atlantic to the Pacific*. Delta, UT: n.p. 1957.

Lyman, William H., Parowan, Utah, letter published in *Utah Historical Quarterly* 10 (1942).

Lythgoe, Dennis. "Physician/Plural Wife Was Real Pioneer in Women's Rights." *Deseret News*, March 3, 1991.

Macdonald, Amelia Peart. *Life Sketch of my Mother, Phebe Amelia Richards Peart*. Filed with Daughters of Utah Pioneers, 1960. Also published in "Mormon Midwives," *Utah Historical Quarterly* 10, nos. 1–4 (1942): 117.

Mackey, Marie W. "Up the rugged hill of Knowledge: Romania Pratt Penrose," *Heroines of the Restoration* (Salt Lake City: Bookcraft, 1997).

Matthews, Miriam. *The Negro in California from 1781–1910: An Annotated Bibliography*, typescript, 1944.

McCrimmon, Elizabeth Cannon. *Dr. Martha Hughes Cannon, Journal Entry*, archived by Daughters of Utah Pioneers (1944), 1–4.

Morril, Lourie Meeks, "Biography of Mary Jane McCleave Meeks." Compiled for Daughters of Utah Pioneers, December 1960.

Mungan, Donna. *The Life and Times of Biddy Mason: From Slavery to Wealthy California Land Owner*. Los Angeles: MC Printing Company, 1976.

Murphy, Miriam B. "The Greek Midwife Magerou." *History Blazer*, (February 1996): 2.

Nichols, Jeffrey D. "Courageous Emma Lee Endured Many Hardships in Pioneer Utah," *History Blazer* (July 1995).

Noall, Claire. *Guardians of the Hearth: Utah's Pioneer Midwives and Women Doctors*. Bountiful, UT: Horizon Publishers, 1974.

———. "Mormon Midwives," *Utah Historical Quarterly* 10 (1942), 84–144.

Oldroyd, Leila H., Catherine Mary Meicklejohn, and Todd Oldroyd. *Women of Faith and Fortitude*. Submitted to International Society of Daughters of Utah Pioneers, November 3, 2004.

Papanikolas, Helen Zeese. "Magerou, the Greek Midwife," *Utah Historical Quarterly* 39 (1970).

Penrose, Esther Romania Bunnell Pratt. *Memoirs, 1881*. Church History Library, MS 48111.

Peterson, JoAnn A., ed. *The Life Story of Martha Hughes (Paul) Cannon, July 1, 1857–July 10, 1932*. (Whittier, CA, 1985).

Pinkney, Andrea Davis. *Let it Shine: Stories of Black Women Freedom Fighters* New York: Harcourt, 2000.

Platt, Mrs. Francis B. "Interview." In "Mormon Midwives." *Utah Historical Quarterly* 10 (1942): 137.

Platt, Henriette Hope Russell. "A Pioneer History of My Mother Lucy Pratt Russell." Submitted to the International Society of Daughters of Utah Pioneers.

Porter, F. L. "Record of the United Order." *Utah Historical Quarterly* 10 (1942): 189.

Rainey, Brandi. "Female Pioneer Doctors: Women's Legacy in the History of Utah Medicine," *Pioneer* (Autumn 2000): 9–10.

Rawich, George, ed. *The American Slave: A Composite Autobiography*, supp. ser. 2, vol. 1. Westport, CT: Greenwood, 1979.

Richardson, Gladwell. "Doctor Grandma French." *Frontier Times* 41, no. 4 (1967).

Rose, Blanche E. "Early Utah Medical Practice: Women Doctors." *Utah Historical Quarterly* 10 (1942): 27–32.

Robinson, Deidre. *Open Hands, Open Heart: The Story of Biddy Mason.* Gardenia, CA: Sly Fox Publishing Company, 1998.

Russell, Lucy Pratt. *Family Papers, 1837–1937*, Church History Library, MS 418010.

Schindler, Harold. "Sculptor's Subject a Tall Order." *Salt Lake Tribune*, July 16, 1995.

Schricker, J. Louis, Jr., M.D. F.A.C.S. *Martha Hughes Cannon.* International Society of Daughters of Utah Pioneers, unknown date, 1–7.

Shaw, Anna Hermina. "History of My Mother: Netta Anna Furrer Cardon." Compiled by Isabelle E. K. Wilson. International Society of Daughters of Utah Pioneers. Collected and filed, 1963.

Sherr, Lynn and Jurate Kazickas. *Susan B. Anthony Slept Here: A Guide to American Women's Landmarks.* Random House, 1994.

Shipp, Ellis Reynolds, *Autobiography of Ellis Reynolds Shipp M.D.* Compiled by Ellis Shipp Musser. Salt Lake City, Utah, 1961.

———. *Life Lines—Poems.* Salt Lake City: Skelton Publishing Company, 1910.

———. Talk given to Daughters of the Utah Pioneers, Camp Nine. Salt Lake City, UT, June 1832, 5–9.

———. *While Others Slept: Autobiography and Journal of Ellis Reynolds Shipp, M.D.* Salt Lake City: Bookcraft, 1962.

Shipp, Winston B. *Women of Faith and Fortitude: Ellis Reynolds Shipp.* Salt Lake City: Daughters of Utah Pioneers, 1982, 14.

Sims, Oscar L. "Profile of Biddy Mason." *Epic Lives of One Hundred Black Women Who Made a Difference.* Detroit: Visible Ink Press, 1993.

"Slavery in California." *Journal of Negro History* 3 (1918): 33–54.

Smart, Donna Toland Smart, ed. "Mormon Midwife: The Diaries of Patty Bartlett Sessions. Salt Lake City: Utah University Press, 1997, 342.

Smith, Barbara B., and Blythe Darlyn Thatcher, eds. "Up the Rugged Hill of Knowledge: Romania Pratt Penros," in *Heroines of the Restoration*. Salt Lake City: Bookcraft, 1997.

Smith, Jessie Carney, ed. *Notable Black American Women*. Detroit: Gale Research, 1992.

Smith, Joseph F., Jr., and John J. Stewart. *The Life of Joseph Fielding Smith*. Salt Lake City: The Church of Jesus Christ of Latter-day Saints, 1972.

Smith, Mary Heathman. *Midwife Log, 1878–1895*, Church History Library, MS 403.

Smith, William G. *Biographical Sketch of Mary Heathman Smith*. Compiled by Carol Widdison. Daughters of Utah Pioneers, April 1991. Also in Church History Library, MS 12634.

Stegner, Wallace. *The Gathering of Zion: The Story of the Mormon Trail*. New York: McGraw-Hill, 1964.

Tanaka, Julynn Ann. *Biography of Hilda Anderson Erickson: Utah's Last Surviving Pioneer*. Salt Lake City: Church History Library, 1997.

Thomas, Jennie Skolfield. *History of My Mother Jane Wilkie Manning Skolfield*. Archived by the International Society of Daughters of Utah Pioneers (1959), 3.

Thurman, Sue Bailey. *Pioneers of Negro Origin in California*. San Francisco: Acme Publishers, 1952.

Utah State Historical Society. J. Cecil Alter, ed. *Utah Historical Quarterly* 10 (1942):20.

"Vigdis Bjornsdottir." David's Icelandic Site, accessed February 22, 2011, www.tahicelandersdavid.com.

Wangsgaard, Stanley. "Mary Heathman Smith, Huntsville Midwife." *Ogden Valley Historian* (September 15, 2002), 21–22.

Waters, Christine Croft. "*Pioneering Physicians in Utah, 1847–1900*." Master's thesis, University of Utah, 1977.

Wells, Emmeline B. "Centennial of President Zina D. H. Young." *Relief Society Magazine* 8, no. 3 (March 1921), 133.

Wheeler, B. Gordon. *Black California: The History of the African American in the Golden State.* New York: Hippocrene Books, 1993.

Whitlet, Colleen. *Worth Their Salt: Notable but Often Unnoted Women of Utah.* Utah State University Press, 1996.

Williams, Jean Kinney. *Bridget "Biddy" Mason: From Slave to Businesswoman.* Minneapolis: Compass Point Books, 2005.

Wilcox, Elizabeth S. "Interview." Published in *Utah Historical Quarterly* 10 (1942), 119.

Wilcox, Genevieve. "Interview." Published in *Utah Historical Quarterly* 10 (1942), 124.

Wood, Joseph S. "The Mormon Settlement in San Bernadino, 1851–1857." PhD diss., University of Utah, Salt Lake City, Utah, 1967.

Wood, Josephine Catherine Chatterly. "Journal of Josephine Catherine Chatterly Wood." *Utah Historical Quarterly* 10 (1942), 128–136.

Workman, Clarissa B. "History of Emma Batchelor," submitted by Lucille M. Bevant, archived by the International Society of Daughters of Utah Pioneers.

Young, Kimball. *Isn't One Wife Enough?* Westport, CT: Greenwood Press, 1970.

Young, Zina, *Zina Diantha Huntington Young Diary 1844–1847,* typescript. Salt Lake City: Church Archives, The Church of Jesus Christ of Latter-day Saints, 310.

* All scriptures quoted are from the King James Version of the Holy Bible

PRAISE FOR
ZION'S HOPE

"*Zion's Hope* is a wonderful book with so much evidence for selfless sacrifice among these noble women. I am amazed at their dedication and . . . am grateful to share some of their heritage simply by trying to follow in their footsteps."

—Dr. E. William Parker
OB/GYN who has delivered over 6,000 babies

"Encouraging and Inspirational! *Zion's Hope* encourages and inspires with stories of early midwives in Utah—reminding us of a loving God who created women's bodies for the beautiful birth process. The examples of faith, devotion, consecration, and service in the lives of these pioneer women and their families are worthy of emulation."

—Thea Boden
Mother of seven, Orem, Utah